The Amazon Way

14 Leadership Principles Behind the World's Most Disruptive Company

John Rossman

ISBN: 1499296770
ISBN 13: 9781499296778
Library of Congress Control Number: 2014905059
LCCN Imprint Name: CreateSpace Independent
Publishing Platform, North Charleston, S.C.

Contents

Foreword

by Julie Weed

To hundreds of millions of people around the world, Amazon.com is a household name. But few know the inside story of how Amazon became the seemingly unstoppable powerhouse it is today. What was it like to work there as the company blossomed, successfully opening up more than a dozen new retail categories and outgrowing its headquarters in downtown Seattle? What made it possible for Amazon to transition from an online retailer to the inventor of a selling platform for all kinds of other companies and products, exponentially increasing its own reach and becoming the go-to store for almost any imaginable consumer product?

John Rossman was there during that critical period, and in this book, he'll tell you how it about the leadership culture behind it all.

From the beginning, starting with his 1997 Letter to Shareholders, Amazon founder Jeff Bezos has focused on the long term, on reinventing the customer experience, and on perfecting the technologies that would make it all possible. Over time, a set of leadership principles emerged and were used to make smart strategic decisions and accurate everyday choices.

These principles aren't slogans printed on wall posters and coffee mugs. They are lived and breathed every day by Amazonians from the CEO on down. They are principles that other companies, small or large, may just want to adopt.

Every department at Amazon, from the mailroom to the tech team responsible for the Kindle book delivery system, has a year-over-year improvement plan. How will we get better? What does the customer want from us? How can we use new technology to improve the customer experience? Lots of companies aspire to innovate, to create more value for customers. At Amazon, making that happen is ingrained in the corporate psyche. And this innovation mentality is just one of the principles that have enabled the company to outgrow its competitors and consistently surprise the best of the business world.

Now you can journey back in time to Amazon's early days of crazy growth, continual reinvention, and wild (but never thoughtless) experimentation. John Rossman offers both an insider's view of Amazon's history and an insightful analysis of the leadership principles that have helped Jeff Bezos own America's shopping list.

Just turn the page.

Julie Weed is a freelance writer who covers the world of business for The New York Times *and other publications. Her national best-seller,* All I Really Need to Know in Business I Learned at Microsoft, *has been published in 12 languages.*

Introduction

It is January, 2003. With less than a year under my belt as Amazon.com's director of merchant integration, I am still considered the new guy on the block. At the moment, I am sitting in a conference room in the company's Seattle headquarters, surrounded by what's called the S-Team, a group that includes Amazon's 20 most senior executives, and I happen to be the center of attention. Unfortunately, this is because the founder and CEO, Jeff Bezos, is frustrated.

"The answer to that question begins with *a number!*" he roars.

All eyes had turned in my direction when Jeff asked me a deceptively simple question: "How many merchants have launched since the first of the year?"

The question had puzzled me, since at the moment there simply aren't any third-party sellers—"merchants," in Jeff's parlance—to launch, which was out of my direct control. A bit apologetically, I responded, "Well, you see, as of right now—"

Before I could finish, Jeff had erupted. "The answer to that question begins with *a number!*"

Jeff's reputation for pyrotechnic displays of emotion is already part of his legend. Jeff Bezos doesn't worry about your feelings; he doesn't give a damn whether or not you're having a good day. He only cares about results—and they'd better be the right results. Everyone who joins Amazon.com understands this; it's part of the deal. But this is the first time I've found myself at the business end of his double-barreled fury, and I'm more than a little shell-shocked by the experience. I hesitate, frantically juggling possible responses in my head. Finally, taking a big gulp, I offer the simple answer he is asking for: "Six, but ..."

Jeff pounces like a lion tearing into the soft underbelly of its kill. "That is the most pathetic answer I have ever heard!"

The ensuing rant is neither a simple exercise in humiliation nor some sort of power play designed to reinforce Jeff's status as the alpha dog of Amazon.com. It's an educational exercise that uses my situation as an opportunity to set an example and to transmit a series of cultural, strategic, and operational messages to the leaders of the company. The lecture is classic Jeff because, despite its thunderous volume and tone, it contains valuable lessons about the principles that define Amazon.com. In the next five minutes, Jeff touches on a half dozen of these principles as he describes my shortcomings in painful detail. I am chastised for my failure to sufficiently obsess over the customer, for not taking complete ownership of my project and its outcomes, for not setting higher standards for myself and my team, for not thinking big enough, for not possessing a bias for action, and for not being firmly and vocally self-critical when it was clear my performance was lacking. Throughout, I am pinned to my chair as if by a hurricane-force gale.

When Jeff's rant finally ends, he simply leaves the room without another word and, just like that, the S-Team meeting has ended. As I allow myself to start breathing again, processing what has just happened, I notice that many of the other senior leaders are smiling at me—and not unkindly. A few make a point of congratulating me as they gather their things and file out of the conference room.

"He likes you," one explains with a pat on the shoulder. "He wouldn't take the time to embarrass you like that if he didn't."

Introduction

In a fog, I stumble from the conference room, clutching my notes and half-wondering how it is that I am still employed. "How can anyone possibly withstand the white-hot crucible of Jeff's expectations?" I wonder.

The key, of course, is right in front of my nose. In fact, it's publicly available on the Amazon.com site if you know where to look.[1] And in that 2003 meeting, Jeff was all but hitting me over the head with it: The 14 leadership principles that drive Amazon, from top to bottom. I've edited a bit of the language of the leadership principles for readability.

How has Jeff Bezos built a company, a culture, and a legacy that meet his highest standards? Unlike in most organizations, Amazon's leadership principles are not simply suggested guidelines for new hires or empty verbiage from a mission statement buried in the employee manual. They are core tenets on which company leaders are rigorously rated during their annual performance reviews and self-evaluations. In fact, as a leader or potential leader at Amazon.com, you are expected to record concrete examples of how you embody the 14 leadership principles and to be prepared to cite them upon request.

This book is not a tell-all story of my time at Amazon.com. The fact is that, after I moved on to my current position as a managing director at the consulting firm Alvarez & Marsal, I didn't expect to think much about my years at Amazon.com at all. Funny thing, though: as I began to tackle the wide range of challenges presented by my clients in fields from technology and manufacturing to retail and even philanthropy, I found myself frequently referencing strategies, management techniques, and approaches I had experienced at Amazon.com. At first, I didn't even notice I was doing it. Then a colleague of mine said, "You know, you should really write those down."

"Write what down?" I asked.

"All those lessons from Amazon. You're constantly using them. Might as well capture them all in one place. I bet people would find them interesting. I know I would."

I decided to give it a try. I began roughly outlining the concepts, lessons, strategies, and approaches I'd learned, observed, and practiced at Amazon. To my surprise, although seven years had passed since I'd left the company, the content was all right there at the surface, ready to be transcribed and organized. Before long, I realized that the lessons had grouped themselves into 14 leadership principles.

What makes Amazon's principles so unforgettable—even for a company alumnus who'd made no special effort to recall them? The answer has a lot to do with why Jeff Bezos was so livid at my status report on merchant integration in that 2003 S-Team meeting. Amazon's leaders work hard to make their thinking very clear—to be clear not only about *what* they decide, but about precisely *why* they decide as they do. This quest for clarity has created an organization whose actions are based on a specific philosophy and a consistent set of values and principles. It's a way to get the details right and scale the business successfully—something Amazon. com has arguably done better than any other company in history.

Encouraged by my colleague's suggestion, I decided to turn my notes into a book. I've deliberately kept it short and, I hope, enjoyable to read. A few years ago, I read with interest a story of a 52-year-old Slovenian athlete who decided—who knows why?—to swim the length of the Amazon River. He survived 3,272 miles of exhaustion, sunburn, delirium, and piranhas to set a world record for distance swimming. While his journey up the Amazon was an amazing feat, I don't want yours to feel like a grueling test of endurance. Although the story of Amazon.com is a continent-spanning tale of growth, innovation, and steadily-increasing influence, the company's strategies, management techniques, and approaches are both simple to understand and difficult to emulate. So I've strived to present them as clearly and directly as possible. Instead of a marathon swim through the muddy currents of business think, consider this book a riverboat tour with 14 stops—one for each of the leadership principles.

Sit back and relax. I hope you enjoy the ride.

1. Obsess Over the Customer

Leaders at Amazon start with the customer and work backwards, seeking continually to earn and keep the customer's trust. Although leaders pay attention to their competitors, they obsess over their customers.

Jeff Bezos's customer obsession is really something beyond a mere obsession—it's a psychosis that has generated many of his most vitriolic tirades or, more often, sarcastic comments at Amazon associates who have fallen short of his own standard for customer service. It stems from Jeff's unique ability to put himself in the customer's position, deduce his or her unspoken needs and wants, and then develop a system that will meet those needs and wants better than anyone else has ever done.

This approach to business is at the core of Jeff's genius. Long before social media revolutionized the retail world with its vast, transparent networks linking companies, customers, prospects, and detractors; long before companies like Zappos.com made customer service the foundation of their business model; and even long before Jeff had fully realized his own vision for Amazon.com, he had profoundly internalized two truths about customer service:

- When a company makes a customer unhappy, she won't tell a friend, or two, or three . . . she'll tell many, many more; and
- The best customer service is *no* customer service—because the best experience happens when the customer never has to ask for help at all.

Of course, an actual business model that doesn't require *any* customer service is about as realistic as a perpetual motion machine. But very early in the Internet revolution, Jeff saw that the online retail model raised the bar of what was possible. He long recognized that the biggest threat to the customer experience was human beings getting involved and mucking things up. The logical corollary was that the key to creating the most pleasant, frictionless customer experience possible was minimizing human involvement through process innovation and technology.

(Of course, Amazon still needs human beings. Throughout this book, we will discuss the techniques Jeff developed to help him hire, evaluate, and retain the very best talent in the world. But Amazon's goal has always been to minimize the time and energy its talented people must spend on routine service interactions, freeing them to innovate new ways to delight the customer.)

Jeff's insight led to some counterintuitive tactics. Back in the late 1990s, Amazon.com made it intentionally difficult for customers to find the customer service number, which momentarily confused some observers who thought this reflected an attitude of disdain for customers. But those customers quickly realized that Jeff's engineers had created a robust technology that enabled them to deal with their services requests almost instantaneously with no human intervention. This wasn't as difficult as it might sound. After all,

98 percent of all customer questions at a retailer like Amazon boil down to, "Where is my stuff?" An online tracking tool that lets the customer following his shipment from the warehouse to his front door eliminates the need for a large, costly call center and the vast amounts of organizational friction it generates.

Jeff believed that people don't actually like to talk to customer service representatives. He was right. All he had to do was provide the data, tools and retrain customers to answer their own questions. Now customers have come to expect and demand effortless self-service customer care technology, a concept explained by Bill Price and David Jaffe in their 2008 book, *The Best Service is No Service*: The more frictionless the experience, the more loyal the customer and the lower the control costs. And this includes marketing and advertising costs as well. Price and Jaffe explain, "Amazon has enjoyed a 90 percent reduction in its CPO [contacts per order], meaning that it could keep customer care costs (headcount and associated operational expenses) flat with a 9x increase in orders (revenues), a major contributor to the company's profitability beginning in 2002."[1]

The best customer service *just works*, without effort—producing incredible benefits both for customers and for the company that serves them. Take, for example, Amazon.com's revolutionary Free Shipping program, launched in November, 2000. It was originally called the "Free Super Saver Shipping Offer" and was good only for orders over $100. Instead of paying for advertising, Amazon.com pumped its money into free shipping, which resulted in customer-driven word of mouth, the world's most effective (and cheapest) form of advertising. This created a virtuous cycle: by sacrificing short-term financials for customer benefit, the strategy drove long-term competitive and financial benefit. "In the old world, you devoted 30 percent of your time to building a great service and 70 percent of your time to shouting about it," Jeff explained. "In the new world, that inverts."[2]

At the time, free shipping seemed like a wildly radical and risky strategy. Now customers expect it. In fact, most people assume that companies will pay for return shipping as well—just one of the ways Amazon has raised the bar on customer service for countless businesses.

The Virtuous Cycle Goes Fractal: The Flywheel Effect

Allen Mandelbrot founded the field of fractal mathematics, which studies (among other phenomena) how patterns in nature have a tendency to repeat themselves at different scales—for example, the way spiral galaxies resemble whorling sea shells which in turn resemble tiny unfurling fern fronds. In a similar fractal fashion, the virtuous cycle is replicated throughout Amazon.com at macro and micro levels. It generates a set of self-reinforcing energies that continue to flow even when the energy source is discontinuous—much like a flywheel, which is the favorite metaphor for this phenomenon at Amazon.com.

Here's a macro example of how the flywheel effect works (see Figure 1.1). Jeff doesn't focus on margins. He's more focused on free cash flow—that is, the cash that a company is able to generate after laying out the money required to maintain or expand its asset base. Why? Because he believes the Internet's potential for growth is gargantuan and still fundamentally unexploited. To Jeff, the year is 1889 and the

Oklahoma Land Rush is on—or, as he likes to put it, it's still Day One of the Internet. So he's ready to slash prices and create programs like free shipping to cultivate customer loyalty and drive sales growth toward the unimaginable heights he foresees. Then he invests the revenues generated back into "the holy trinity": price, selection, and availability (more on this later).

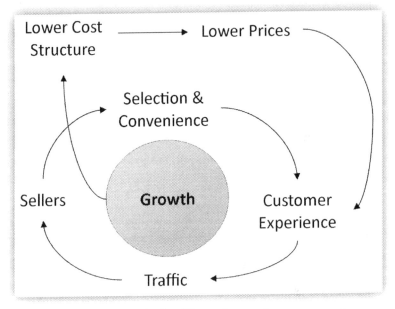

Figure 1.1. The flywheel effect: How an improved customer experience and customer growth feed one another in a virtuous cycle.

Sometimes, the lever you need to pull in order to create the flywheel effect can be sticky and difficult to budge. The effort involved can be costly, even painful. Jeff and the companies' stockholders had to be willing to sacrifice a lot at the very beginning so long as the customer experience was the primary beneficiary. Not every CEO has the stomach this requires. But Jeff's readiness to pay the price has produced much of Amazon's success.

In July, 1999, Jeff decided to move Amazon into the electronics business. The company was making a lot of money on book sales, but he knew that the push into electronics would be the first big step into a limitless world of new markets. Critics doubted it would work. Many said that customers needed to physically see and touch the equipment in a showroom and learn how to operate it with help from trained professionals. These critics—including many at leading manufacturers like Sony as well as analysts on Wall Street—needed to be convinced that Amazon.com was capable of selling electronics at a high volume and as an "Everyday Low Price" leader. Until they were won over, Amazon's electronics business would face tough sledding, including a cost structure much too high for the modest sales it would initially generate.

Many retailers aren't willing to operate in the red for a while. Jeff was. And while it was ugly for a number of quarters (seemingly validating the warnings of the doubters on Wall Street), by providing enough information and a frictionless return process, Amazon.com eventually built the type of volume that convinced the vendors and big-name manufacturers that people would buy complicated technology online. Jeff had wagered that his customers were intelligent enough to figure out electronics on their own—and he had won.

Once that flywheel was engaged, the energy generated was huge. Amazon.com's success in the electronics market kicked off a virtuous cycle of expanding e-commerce markets that continues to spin to this day.

The Holy Trinity

Amazon.com's strategy includes great pricing on virtually every product it sells. But the strategy is not just about price. A wide selection and fast, convenient availability with great delivery and service are equally critical elements of long-term customer needs. Price, selection, and availability . . . these are the three durable and universal customer desires that Amazon thinks of as its holy trinity.

Offer everything, get it cheaper, and make it more easily available. Fashions, tastes, product types, and form factors change, but the holy trinity won't. That's why Jeff Bezos embraced this strategy from the earliest days of Amazon. Here's an excerpt from his very first letter to Amazon's shareholders in 1997:

> From the beginning, our focus has been on offering our customers compelling value. We realized that the Web was, and still is, the World Wide Wait. Therefore, we set out to offer customers something they simply could not get any other way, and began serving them with books. We brought them much more selection than was possible in a physical store (our store would now occupy 6 football fields), and presented it in a useful, easy-to-search, and easy-to-browse format in a store open 365 days a year, 24 hours a day. We maintained a dogged focus on improving the shopping experience, and in 1997 substantially enhanced our store. We now offer customers gift certificates, 1-Click(SM) shopping, and vastly more reviews, content, browsing options, and

recommendation features. We dramatically lowered prices, further increasing customer value. Word of mouth remains the most powerful customer acquisition tool we have, and we are grateful for the trust our customers have placed in us. Repeat purchases and word of mouth have combined to make Amazon.com the market leader in online bookselling.[3]

Price, selection, and availability—all the elements of the holy trinity are there. Incidentally, Jeff has attached this original 1997 shareholder letter to the back of every shareholder letter he has written since. And he repeats the same mantra every chance he gets. In 2004, I accompanied Jeff when he gave a talk to the leadership team at Target, the large retailer. Jeff's message: He could never imagine a day when the customer would want higher prices, less selection, or a more complex and difficult transaction process. The holy trinity is eternal and must never be forgotten.

Let's take a closer look at the three elements of the holy trinity and consider how Amazon has built its business around each one.

Price. Amazon's low-price strategy is well documented. For nearly two decades, Jeff has proven that he is willing to make less on an item—or an entire line of products—in the short term to guarantee the long-term growth of the business. Yet Jeff's obsession with pricing knows no bounds. Here's an example:

During my years at Amazon, everyone understood that our goal was to be an Everyday Low Price leader. To do that, we had to make sure our prices matched those of our image competitors—Walmart, Best Buy, and Target. During one

S-Team meeting, someone opined, "If the retailer with the lowest price doesn't have the item in stock, then we shouldn't match price. Why bleed the margin for no reason?"

Jeff immediately objected, pointing out how this might backfire. If customers saw that our price was higher, they'd grudgingly buy an item unavailable elsewhere—but the transaction would leave a bitter taste in their mouth that they would associate with Amazon.com. Jeff rejected the idea of protecting our profit margin, emphasizing that what really mattered was what customers were thinking.

Of course, a low-margin pricing strategy is constantly under siege. Most recently, the pressure has been coming from some very unlikely competitors—brick and mortar retailers. An analyst for BB&T Capital Markets made waves in the media when he reported that the prices charged by retailer Bed, Bath & Beyond on a representative "basket" of thirty items had fallen from 9 percent higher than those charged by Amazon (in early 2012) to 6.5 percent lower than Amazon's (as of August 2013).[4] Other traditional retailers, such as Best Buy, are offering guarantees to match Amazon's pricing. Thanks to factors such as falling real estate prices, the gradual leveling of the sales tax playing field between online and offline retailers, and the greater leeway to reduce prices among old-school merchants with healthy profit margins (like those currently enjoyed by Bed, Bath & Beyond), Amazon's once-huge price advantage over brick-and-mortar retailers is fading. How Amazon will respond to this intensified competition is one of the big questions for the company's future.

Selection. From the beginning, Jeff Bezos's goal was to make Amazon a source for virtually anything a customer might want to buy, starting with an unmatched assortment of books and other media products and then expanded to include a practically unlimited array of goods.

Of course, trying to become "the everything store" (as described in the title of Brad Stone's excellent 2013 book about Amazon's history) is far from easy. When Jeff couldn't figure out how to organically scale Amazon.com to provide the vast assortment of products he envisioned, the idea of the third-party marketplace was formed. The world was full of people already selling everything under the sun. Jeff hired me to figure out a way to cohabitate with them under the umbrella of the Amazon.com brand (see Chapter 7, "Think Big"). Long story short, we eventually figured out how to sell everything without carrying a huge load of inventory or the risk that goes with it.

Today, the scale at which Amazon.com operates is nearly infinite, providing a richness and variety of customer experience that would have seemed impossible a few years ago. What are you looking for? Uranium? Check. A fresh, whole rabbit? Sure. Bacon-shaped Band-Aids? Roger that. If you can imagine it, chances are it can be purchased on Amazon. com. And the more out-of-the-ordinary products customers discover when they browse Amazon's site, the more they make it their default location for any shopping they want to do, making the flywheel spin even faster.

Availability. Any time Amazon takes a customer order, it offers a projected arrival time for the package using the Amazon-speak term "the Promise." Why the heavy language? Because Jeff knows that in business, there are heavy consequences for those who don't have an item or can't get it to a customer quickly. Woe to those who fail to honor any element of the holy trinity—including convenient, timely availability.

One year, we ordered 4,000 pink iPods from Apple for Christmas. In mid-November, an Apple rep contacted us to say, "Problem—we can't make Christmas delivery. They're transitioning from a disk drive to a hard drive memory in the iPods, and they don't want to make any more using the old technology. Once we get the new ones made, we'll get you your four thousand. But it won't be in time for the holiday."

Other retailers would have simply apologized to their customers for the failure to deliver a product on time. That wasn't going to fly at Amazon.com. We were not the kind of company that ruined people's Christmas because of a lack of availability—not under any circumstances. So we went out and bought 4,000 pink iPods *at retail* and had them all shipped to our Union Street office. Then we hand-sorted them, repacked them, and shipped them to the warehouse to be packaged and sent to our customers. It killed our margins on those iPods, but it enabled us to keep our promise to our customers.

During the next weekly business review, we had to explain to Jeff what we were doing and why. He just nodded approvingly and said, "I hope you'll get in touch with Apple and try to get our money back from the bastards." Ultimately, Apple did grudgingly split the cost difference with us. But even if they hadn't, it still would have been the right thing for Amazon to do.

Serving the Customer: The Andon Cord

The Andon Cord is not a unique Amazon concept; it is an idea borrowed from Japanese lean manufacturing. My Amazon colleague, Clifford Cancelosi, was in the room when the concept was originally adapted for use at Amazon. It's a lean manufacturing principle most famously used in car manufacturing. Say you're working in a busy Toyota assembly plant, and you notice that the widget you're installing doesn't fit or is broken. You immediately reach up and pull the Andon Cord, stopping the assembly line and forcing an inspection so that the defect can be ferreted out quickly. As consultant Todd Wangsgard explains, "The andon cord is literally a cord that workers can pull – a cord they should pull – any time something in the manufacturing process goes wrong that would compromise the quality of the product or safety of the people. The line stops immediately."[5]

The Amazon version of the Andon Cord started with a conversation about a customer care problem during a weekly business review. The issue centered on the way mistakes made by one set of employees—those working in the retail group—were creating headaches for a different set—those in the customer care department. "When the people in the retail group don't provide the right data for the customer or enter a product description that's inaccurate," the head of customer care explained, "the customer is disappointed with the purchase. And that means they call customer care, which lands us with the hassle of refunding the product."

We discussed the problem and left the folks in the retail group with some action items intended to fix it. But a couple of weeks later, customers reported that nothing had gotten better.

Frustrated, the customer care group took matters into their own hands, creating their own version of the Andon Cord. When customers began complaining about a problem with a product, customer care simply took that product down from the website and sent a message to the retail group that said, in effect, "Fix the defect or you can't sell this product." Needless to say, in the world of retail, halting the sale of a product is a pretty disruptive step—the equivalent of shutting down an automotive assembly line. Yet Jeff was adamant in supporting the system. "If you retail guys can't get it right, you deserve to be punished," he declared.

The story of the Andon Cord underscores yet again the obsession with the customer that permeates Amazon. But it also illustrates the importance—and the challenge—of thinking about *internal* customers. When I was tasked with launching the third-party marketplace, I found it very difficult to get our internal people to think about the third-party sellers with the same amount of passion as shoppers. But for my group, these third-party sellers were customers who deserved to be treated with the same reverence as our website shoppers. The Andon Cord is one way to force people to pay attention to the needs of their internal or external customers—by literally shutting down the business until those needs are met.

Amazon literally has jobs titled "Senior Product Manager, Andon Cord," whose role is to build cross organizational process and systems that detect and "pull the Andon Cord" when defects occur. It's a form of real-time instrumentation to detect errors and force teams to fix them.[6]

The Voice of the Customer as a Driver of Innovation

In the early days of Amazon, Jeff Bezos would bring an empty chair into meetings as a constant reminder to his team that the customer, even though she might not be physically present in the room, still needed to be constantly acknowledged and heard. But Amazon also takes unusual steps to ensure that the literal voice of the customer is heard throughout the organization. The goal is to ensure that customer feedback is used to identify, examine, and fix root problems in Amazon's operations. Jeff requires all of his managers to attend two days of call-center training each year. In fact, if you dial into the call center on just the right day, you may even get Jeff himself on the line. In theory, the resulting sense of understanding and empathy for the customer trickles up into the very highest echelons of the organization.

Of course, in the age of blogs, tweets, and Facebook posts, a single customer complaint that goes viral can have a devastating impact. So Jeff has invested millions to construct systems that monitor the online feedback Amazon. com receives from its customers. For example, during my time heading up the third-party marketplace, we established an internal email system that facilitates and monitors conversations with customers and retailers, uses metrics to track customer complaints about third-party retailers, and implements a fulfillment capability (Fulfillment by Amazon) which lets merchants easily leverage Amazon.com's distribution channels.

Jeff's shareholder letter dated April, 2013, describes another example of how the customer experience drives innovation at Amazon:

> We build automated systems that look for occasions when we've provided a customer experience that isn't up to our standards, and those systems

then proactively refund customers. One industry observer recently received an automated email from us that said, "We noticed that you experienced poor video playback while watching the following rental on Amazon Video On Demand: Casablanca. We're sorry for the inconvenience and have issued you a refund for the following amount: $2.99. We hope to see you again soon." Surprised by the proactive refund, he ended up writing about the experience: "Amazon 'noticed that I experienced poor video playback...' And they decided to give me a refund because of that? Wow...Talk about putting customers first."[7]

The history of the company is studded with innovative triumphs driven by customer obsession. Pushing the publishing industry to make books available electronically provided readers with instant gratification at lower prices. Providing unlimited next-day delivery (the Amazon Prime loyalty program) for $79 (now $99) a year drove revenue by drastically reducing the friction involved in online shopping. And Amazon Web Services, the category leader and chief innovator in the field of cloud computing, was based on the idea of offering business customers the same sophisticated online infrastructure technology that Amazon has developed for itself.

Here is a closer look at some of Amazon's biggest customer-driven innovation hits:

Look Inside The Book.™ In 2001, Amazon.com launched this program based on a simple concept—the idea of emulating the bookstore experience by allowing Amazon.com surfers to look at pages inside the book before buying.

Of course, this required Amazon.com to house book content in online form on their site, which raised some questions about whether this would expose book content to piracy. Publishers were worried and skeptical. The program would also be very costly. Each book would have to be scanned digitally and indexed, a huge logistical challenge.

Jeff gave the go-ahead for a large-scale launch, recognizing that this was the only way to see whether it would go over with Amazon's 43 million active customer accounts.[8] The feature debuted with an astonishing 120,000-plus books. The database took up 20 terabytes, which was about 20 times larger than the biggest database that existed anywhere when Amazon.com was founded.

David Risher was Amazon.com's first vice president of product and store development, responsible for growing the company's revenue from $16 million to over $4 billion. He described the strategy behind the launch of "Look Inside the Book" this way: "If we had tried it in a tentative way on a small number of books, say 1,000 or 2,000, it wouldn't have gotten the PR and the customers' perception. There's an X-factor: What will it look like in scale? It's a big investment, and a big opportunity cost. There's a leap of faith. Jeff is willing to take those gambles."[9] Ultimately, the publishers embraced the "Look Inside the Book" program as an asset to sales.

Amazon Prime. Though many people think of Amazon Prime as a shipping program, it's really a very clever loyalty program. When we were coming up with this concept, Jeff referenced airline credit cards—how you never feel like you're being rewarded when you're using one. He wanted to create a loyalty program that provided very tangible benefits. With Prime, the customer is very clear on how they're being rewarded for shopping with Amazon. The benefits started with free two-day shipping; now members also receive monthly e-book rentals on Kindle devices and can stream selected movies and television shows for no extra charge beyond Prime membership annual fees.

Since its inception in February 2005, Amazon Prime has become an increasingly important part of Amazon.com's broader strategy to retain customers and get them to spend more time and money on its services and products. Because they pay $79 per year to join, Amazon Prime members use the service more frequently. And Amazon Prime continues to up customer expectation. Amazon may soon introduce free same-day delivery in certain urban areas.

‹▲›

In the end, Amazon.com's strategy for remaining the world's most customer-focused retail company in the years to come leans heavily on another leadership principle: a bias for action (see Chapter 8). Rarely do you find Jeff Bezos reacting to a competitor's initiative. In his mind, it's much preferable to launch a new innovation based on customer needs and experience and force your competitors to react—even if that innovation struggles or fails.

"If you're competitor-focused, you have to wait until there is a competitor doing something," Jeff explains. "Being customer-focused allows you to be more pioneering."[10] Or, as he put it in a 2009 *Fast Company* interview, "There are two ways to extend a business. Take inventory of what you're good at and extend out from your skills. Or determine what your customers need and work backward, even if it requires learning new skills."[11]

2. Take Ownership of Results

Leaders at Amazon are owners. They think long term, and they don't sacrifice long-term value for short-term results. They never say, "That's not my job." They act on behalf of the entire company, not just their own team.

Whenever I discuss the principle of ownership, I think about a famous story in Amazon company lore about a Christmas party early in the life of Amazon which was held at a rented facility in downtown Seattle. When the employees responsible for setup realized they didn't have a stand for the Christmas tree, someone decided to nail its trunk directly to the wooden floor. "What the hell?" they thought. "We're just renting the place."

Jeff, always on the lookout for symbolic gestures to drive home his principles, pounced on the incident. For years, he used this unfortunate solution to highlight the shortcomings of the renter's mentality. "Owners would never nail a tree into the floor."

One of the biggest mistakes you can make as a leader at Amazon.com is sacrificing long-term value for short-term results. Jeff wants his people to approach every business situation as an owner, not a renter.

Of course, Amazon.com enjoys the luxury of a CEO who can think about investments with a horizon that spans years, even decades. Why? Because he still owns more than 87 million shares of the company he founded—approximately 20 percent.[1] Most public companies must respond to the quarterly demands for steady growth in sales, profits, and stock value from the board, the shareholders, and Wall Street. Amazon.com is able to place long bets and nurture them to maturity without as much focus on short-term results. When you look at business opportunities through a lens that's in multiple years or longer, suddenly buying *The Washington Post* may not seem like such a crazy idea. And from the get-go, Jeff has sold investors on this idea of the long-term. That's partially why Amazon gets very different—and much higher—stock valuations than other companies. It's also why investing in scale is so vital to Amazon.com.

Amazon isn't the only company to discover this secret. If you're looking for reliable indicators of enterprise value, take a look at the tenure of the leadership team. Successful organizations with long-term strategic visions tend to have a very low turnover rate at the top. The key, of course, is balancing a culture of long-term commitments with the need to deliver short-term excellence. You want a patient CEO, but you don't want an extremely patient workforce. Maintaining an atmosphere of urgency (see Chapter 8, "Bias for Action") is crucial. The best way to achieve that balance is with a sense of shared ownership. Amazon.com's culture rewards people who plead passionately for their projects or ideas and are empowered to respectfully challenge decisions. In other words, people who give a damn about what they're working on—and own results.

How does Jeff build and maintain this sense of ownership among his team members? One way is by hiring the right people. The company has built an effective and scalable system for recruiting, managing, and developing high-performing talent (see Chapter 5, "Hire and Develop the Best").

Another way is by instilling a sense of accountability throughout every stratum of the organization. As co-owners of Amazon.com, every employee must be unflinching in his accountability and honesty. The highest level of customer service is impossible to achieve without a high degree of accountability and a willingness to be direct, open, and honest—especially when things are *not* going well.

During my time at Amazon.com, we had a philosophy called "the open kimono." If you weren't willing to be completely honest about where you, your project, or your numbers stood, then there was simply no chance of attaining your goals. You had to open your kimono and willingly expose the faults, errors, and limitations of your situation. And as I learned in that 2003 S-Team meeting, if you started caveating or waffling about why you were not hitting objectives, Jeff wouldn't hesitate to tear that kimono off for you. I distinctly remember him asking one poor soul who'd been rambling and tergiversating in an effort to explain away some mistake, "Which do you think you are exhibiting—gross stupidity or sheer incompetence?"

When asking for a report on a failed project, all Jeff ever wanted to know was the following: "Here's what didn't work, why it didn't work, and how we're going to change." If a project looked as if it might be heading for disaster, all he wanted to hear was, "We don't think it's going to work, let's try something else." While an honest mea culpa didn't guarantee that Jeff wouldn't pounce, at least it allowed you to retain a certain measure of self-respect . . . and your job. This balance of driving for success and accountability while realizing that some ideas are not going to work lets the organization "fail forward." Sometimes execution is poor, and that is a performance issue. Sometimes the idea is just not quite the right idea, and so you learn, adjust, and move forward.

In *The Everything Store*, Brad Stone examines this culture of unyielding accountability and summarizes how Bezos's incredibly high standards frequently overwhelmed his people: "Many just couldn't take working for Bezos any longer. He demanded more than they could possibly deliver and was extremely stingy with praise. At the same time, many . . . would later marvel at how much they accomplished."[2] Accountability is not painless. But it's the only sure path to achievement.

Amazon's Principles of Ownership

Simply declaring that everyone in the company is an owner and that he or she will be held accountable for decisions and actions is not enough, of course. There are a number of crucial connecting principles that help transform ownership from a vague aspiration into a daily reality.

Yes, It Is Your Job. Amazon.com employees quickly learn that the phrase "That's not my job" is an express ticket to an exit interview. Ownership means not only mastering your domain, but also being willing to go beyond the boundaries of your role whenever it's needed to improve customer experience or fix a problem.

Such boundary-less behavior requires an understanding of details and metrics which goes two to three degrees deeper than normal. It was not uncommon for senior people at Amazon to be able to talk with knowledge and authority about details of a project that was not in their own department, let alone under their direction. It also implies a readiness to speak up and contribute without having to be asked. For example, if you have something valuable to offer in regard to a specific program, you don't wait to be invited to the next meeting about that program—you simply show up.

You Own Your Dependencies. Of course, everyone in business depends on others for success. Those around you—colleagues, team members, outside suppliers and partners, those in other departments that touch your work—contribute essential elements that make you effective. This means that when they let you down, they can also cause you to fail, sometimes miserably.

At Amazon, one of your primary directives is to identify and tenaciously manage every potential business-derailing dependency you have. It is not okay to fail because of a breakdown of dependencies. That's a failure of leadership and, as you've seen, there is not much wiggle room for excuses at Amazon. When called to account for a problem caused in part or in whole by a dependency breakdown, you must be able to say, "I did these things to manage my dependencies. I went above and beyond the reasonable in my efforts to manage them." That means having rock-solid contracts, service-level agreements, and penalties in place as well as continual, active management of communications. You can assume nothing.

In that 2003 S-Team meeting, Jeff broke down the process of managing dependencies in three easy steps (while, of course, yelling and wildly gesticulating like a madman):

1. Whenever possible, take over the dependencies so you don't have to rely on someone else.
2. If that is impossible, negotiate and manage unambiguous and clear commitments from others.
3. Create hedges wherever possible. For every dependency, devise a fallback plan—a redundancy in a supply chain, for example.

Taking absolute responsibility for every possible dependency under your purview is no small task. This is one reason that very few have the rigor, determination, and tenacity to make it in a leadership role at Amazon.com. It is a company of control freaks run by control freaks and lorded over by the king of control freaks. As one ex-engineer famously said, Jeff Bezos is such a control freak he "makes ordinary control freaks look like stoned hippies."[3]

And since your own team is one of the most important dependencies under your authority, your ability to mentor those around you is a key metric during your annual evaluation. That means your success is intrinsically linked to the success your people have acquired over the course of their careers at Amazon.com.

Compensation Rewards Long-Term Thinking. Finally, Amazon incentivizes ownership by designing compensation plans that reward it.

It's well-known that, compared to many Silicon Valley companies that offer lavish salaries and outlandish perks, Amazon likes to run lean. The company doesn't pay for its employees' cell phones, keeps salaries low, and even uses old doors as desks. (Frugality, as I will discuss in Chapter 8, has long been a forcing function for resourcefulness, self-sufficiency, and invention at Amazon.com). But that doesn't mean employees aren't well compensated. Amazon just prefers to reward employees with stock options rather than salary or cash bonuses.

Jeff explains his logic in the 1997 shareholder letter: "We know our success will be largely affected by our ability to attract and retain a motivated employee base, each of whom must think like, and therefore must actually be, an owner."[4] Jeff incentivized us by letting us share in the rewards of company growth. In so doing, he got us constantly thinking about the long term.

The beauty of the ownership principle is that once you've established it in your organization, it works as a flywheel to drive Leadership Principle No. 3: Invent and Simplify.

3. Invent and Simplify

Leaders at Amazon expect and require innovation and invention from their teams and always find ways to simplify the processes they touch. They are externally aware, look for new ideas from everywhere, and are not limited by "not invented here" thinking. And they are willing to innovate fearlessly despite the fact that they may be misunderstood for a long time.

Amazon.com currently sells more goods online than its next 12 biggest competitors combined, including Staples and Walmart.[1] What's more, Amazon.com's sales are growing faster than Internet sales as a whole. When I am asked to explain this unprecedented growth, I go immediately to one of Jeff Bezos's key leadership principles: Amazon.com continues to grow by *inventing and simplifying* every single day.

Jeff understands the same thing that Steve Jobs did: the best design is the simplest. Simple is the key to easy, fast, intuitive, and low-cost. Simple scales much better than complex, which means that simplicity is intrinsically linked to another leadership principle: Think Big (Chapter 7). As a leader at Amazon.com, you are not expected to design and build a new innovation with ten to 100 people in mind. You must design it for millions of customers and tens of thousands

ecosystem partners, such as merchants and developers—
"innovation at scale"—which means truly understanding the
users and innovating with them in mind.

I recently saw an Amazon press release stating that it had
8,000 Amazon Web Services (AWS) partners—companies
that are building solutions and going to market in the cloud
computing business segment. With that kind of partnership
base, Amazon.com leaders are driven to focus on innovation
at scale, achieving repeatable and sustainable organic growth
through new products, services, and business models that
build on the core business. It's a clearly defined, durable, and
oft-repeated directive that is woven into the organizational
DNA from the C-suite to the warehouse.

At Amazon, your job description is never limited to simply running things. No matter what your job, you are expected
to improve on the processes in ways that ultimately enhance
the customer experience and/or lower costs. Amazon.com
engineers, for example, do not consider themselves coders
but rather problem solvers. This mentality promotes big
thinking—game-changing solutions and inventions—rather
than finger-in-the-dike fixes.

Simplification Epitomized: Amazon's Platform Businesses

In the world of business, the term *platform* has come to
refer to a state in which machines interact seamlessly to knit
together complex processes and tasks performed by various
parties. Amazon.com is a platform. It could have stopped
at selling books—the "books platform"—but instead it has
cascaded its scope of service to all forms of consumer items,
and even to the enterprise itself.

My time at Amazon.com made me a big believer in the power of process automation to make workflows simpler and more productive. When a process is automated, it's not only easier to scale but also simpler to measure; while manual effort, even when it begins at a seemingly insignificant level, can evolve into an expensive, non-scalable, and non-real-time capability. That is why automation, algorithms, and technology architecture are the engines behind game-changing platform businesses such as Kindle, Amazon Mechanical Turk, Third-Party Sellers, Fulfillment by Amazon, and Amazon Web Services.

The second page of Jeff's 2011 shareholder letter, entitled "The Power of Invention," is a manifesto about the undeniable impact of data science and computer science on the growth of Amazon's platform businesses:

> Invention comes in many forms and at many scales. The most radical and transformative of inventions are often those that empower others to unleash their creativity—to pursue their dreams. That's a big part of what's going on with Amazon Web Services, Fulfillment by Amazon, and Kindle Direct Publishing. With AWS, FBA, and KDP, we are creating powerful self-service platforms that allow thousands of people to boldly experiment and accomplish things that would otherwise be impossible or impractical. These innovative, large-scale platforms are not zero-sum—they create win-win situations and create significant value for developers, entrepreneurs, customers, authors, and readers.

Amazon Web Services has grown to have thirty different services and thousands of large and small businesses and individual developers as customers. One of the first AWS offerings, the Simple Storage Service, or S3, now holds over 900 billion data objects, with more than a billion new objects being added every day. S3 routinely handles more than 500,000 transactions per second and has peaked at close to a million transactions per second. All AWS services are pay-as-you-go and radically transform capital expense into a variable cost. AWS is self-service: you don't need to negotiate a contract or engage with a salesperson—you can just read the online documentation and get started. AWS services are elastic—they easily scale up and easily scale down.

In just the last quarter of 2011, Fulfillment by Amazon shipped tens of millions of items on behalf of sellers. When sellers use FBA, their items become eligible for Amazon Prime, for Super Saver Shipping, and for Amazon returns processing and customer service. FBA is self-service and comes with an easy-to-use inventory management console as part of Amazon Seller Central. For the more technically inclined, it also comes with a set of APIs [application programming interfaces] so that you can use our global fulfillment center network like a giant computer peripheral.

I am emphasizing the self-service nature of these platforms because it's important for a reason I think is somewhat non-obvious: even well-meaning gatekeepers slow innovation. When a platform is self-service, even the improbable ideas can get tried, because there's no expert gatekeeper ready to say, "that will never work!" And guess what—many of those improbable ideas do work, and society is the beneficiary of that diversity.[2]

Amazon.com's business platforms are enablers. They enable writers and booksellers. They enable people who want to sell to Amazon.com's community. They enable businesses looking to outsource labor. They enable people and companies that want to use Amazon's technology and computing capacity. They enable smaller organizations to enhance their reputations by piggybacking on that of Amazon.com. By empowering entrepreneurs, they enable personal and professional growth for thousands of individuals. Amazon.com's business platforms build virtuous cycles that circulate and expand energy in much the same way as the Amazon flywheel itself.

So if you want to understand how Amazon.com thinks about the principle of invent and simplify, you need to understand the platform opportunity.

As we've noted, technology makes the platform possible. But algorithms, automation, workflow, and technology are only part of how Amazon is inventing and simplifying. More important is the fact that capabilities are designed *from the user backwards*. When we were building the third-party selling business at Amazon.com, creating a great experience for the seller was our goal. Building a simple seller registration process was difficult but essential to achieving that goal, and my job was to push engineering teams to integrate more than 40 different underlying systems to create a seamless and simple workflow for that process.

Willingness to rethink policies, rules, and other assumptions that are widely accepted in the business world is critical. So is asking and answering the question, "If I had to completely automate the process and eliminate *all* manual steps, how would I design it?" Instead of aiming for a ten-percent reduction in friction, push a much more radical rethinking of assumptions; ask "the five whys" (see Chapter 12, "Dive Deep"), and have the willingness to challenge the status quo. This is where all types of resistance, both active and passive, will be experienced, requiring a response from strong executive leadership. Some jobs will be changed, others will be eliminated. For all these reasons, it takes vision, creativity, desire, and courage to carry out the invent-and-simplify principle.

Process vs. Bureaucracy

Notice that the two halves of the principle—invent and simplify—are both equally necessary. Process innovation can be enormously powerful, but when it is practiced without an emphasis on simplicity, the result is bureaucracy—the multiplication of processes for their own sake.

One of the great observations I heard from Jeff came during one of our all-hands meetings, held at a local movie theater. Jeff took a question from an employee about avoiding bureaucracy while still ensuring that certain rules were put in place. Jeff responded with "Good process is absolutely essential. Without defined processes, you can't scale, you can't put metrics and instrumentation in place, you can't manage. But avoiding bureaucracy is essential. Bureaucracy is process run amok."

Jeff understood that A-level performers hate bureaucracy and will leave organizations where it encroaches upon them. By contrast, C- and D-level performers, many of whom typically reside in middle management in any given organization, love bureaucracy because they can hide behind it, acting as gatekeepers and frequently creating the kind of friction that can bog down an entire company. Strong processes with measurable outcomes eliminate bureaucracy and expose underperformers.

So how do you recognize bureaucracy and distinguish it from well-defined process? When the rules can't be explained; when they don't favor the customer; when you can't get redress from a higher authority; when you can't get an answer to a reasonable question; when there is no service-level agreement or guaranteed response time built into the process; or when the rules simply don't make sense—when any of these circumstances occur, the chances are good that bureaucracy is beginning to spread.

I distinctly remember one particular S-Team meeting where Jeff looked east, out across Lake Washington to the Microsoft campus, and told us, "I don't want this place to become a country club." He truly feared that, with success and growth, Amazon would become complacent and bloated like Microsoft; that we would lose our spirit and our desire to take risks; that we would cease to insist on the highest standards and gradually entangle ourselves in a giant ball of red tape. He told us that if we became like Microsoft, we would die. What's worse, he said, it won't be fun to come to work anymore.

As you work to invent and perfect processes, always remember that simplicity is an essential bulwark against the creeping onslaught of bureaucracy.

Other People's Work and The Mechanical Turk

Even Amazon.com can't automate everything. One of my favorite strategies for dealing with this fact is the mobilizing of Other People's Work (OPW). In many cases, the best way to scale an unavoidable residue of manual labor is to enable and motivate other people to do it.

Consider just two of the many tasks that must be done when building an e-commerce website with a virtually infinite array of products: evaluating the quality of a product image and writing clear and accurate product descriptions. Neither can be handled effectively by a computer. Instead of hiring a vast army of people to perform these small but essential and practically endless tasks, Amazon.com handed that task over to its customers and partners. It created a product image management tool that collected customer feedback, allowed customers to compare images, and enabled them to report offensive or irrelevant content. It worked extremely well. Before long, Amazon.com was using OPW to manage other processes that couldn't be automated. Customer reviews, which were controversial when Amazon first introduced them, are a great example of OPW—a way of allowing thousands of Amazon customers to handle the task of describing, rating, and categorizing products for the benefits of millions of other users of the website.

With the right approach, almost every company can find opportunities for OPW. Many of my current clients are finding that letting vendors, customers, or business partners carry out activities for which they have greater motivation and better expertise can be a powerful step toward transforming their businesses while dramatically cutting costs.

Eventually, Amazon's basic OPW concept was retooled into a platform for others to use named Amazon Mechanical Turk. It's an online marketplace that provides businesses access to an on-demand, scalable, flexible army of freelancers they can hire to tackle small, manual tasks. Countless companies use this platform daily to leverage a worldwide employment base and, of course, Amazon.com makes money every time they do.

Third-Party Sellers: Inventing a Platform and Making It Simple

One of the best examples of the principle of invent and simplify is the project that brought me to Amazon in the first place—the development of the third-party seller program.

In late 2001, I was working at a technology start-up and actively looking for the next big thing—both in my own career and in the world of business in general. Jason Child, a colleague of mine from my Arthur Andersen days (he's now the CFO of Groupon), introduced me to Jason Kilar (who later became the founder and CEO of Hulu). They invited me to interview at Amazon.com. The successful candidate, I was told, would lead a business responsible for designing and operating a capability that would allow third parties to sell at Amazon.com.

Over the next two months, I had 23 interviews at Amazon.com. It was, without a doubt, the most exhaustive, intense hiring process I have ever experienced. What we were really doing in these interviews was refining strategy and brainstorming the requirements of a third-party selling business. A precursor already existed. Unfortunately, zShops was largely defined by its horrible customer experience and shoddy inventory. I remember thinking, "Well, the idea is there, but I'm hearing some fairly unbaked plans and expectations."

Eventually, I was hired to lead the launch of the third-party business as Amazon.com's first director of Merchant Integration. I had direct accountability managing all the merchants (a.k.a. sellers) that we were going to bring on board for the opening of the apparel category in late 2002, including brands like Nordstrom, Gap, Eddie Bauer, and Macys. But I was also responsible for making the Amazon.com third-party seller experience just as enjoyable and frictionless as the customer experience. We realized that, without a seller experience culture, the new business would not succeed, and we adopted "seller success" as our mission.

At the time, the dominant third-party selling marketplace was eBay. Their mentality was very laissez-faire; they simply connected buyers with sellers, taking little accountability for customer experience or trust between merchants and shoppers. If you searched for a specific model of camera, you might get pages and pages of individual listings that offered no help in understanding how the items or the offers to sell compared. (Incidentally, eBay has since significantly changed and improved in many of these areas, primarily due to the pressure arising from the success of Amazon.com.)

By contrast, we defined three main design principles that were important to us in building our third-party marketplace business:

1. Present the customer with a single item accompanied by an easy-to-compare list of offers to sell that item. We called this design principle "item authority." Create a single definition of the item, which would allow multiple sellers, including Amazon, to make offers to sell the item. We wanted to create a marketplace where sellers would be competing for the order in a way that worked to the customer's benefit.

2. Make it possible for customers to trust our third-party sellers as much as they trusted Amazon. com itself. We operationalized the concept of "seller trust" in several ways.

3. Provide great seller tools, including multiple selling methods and rich data to help merchants operate their businesses at Amazon.com. For small sellers, simple tools were needed. For more sophisticated high-volume sellers, different types of integrated capabilities should be provided. Documentation, operational metrics, testing environments, and professional service partners should be developed to help sellers be successful while keeping the Amazon team small.

Obviously this was an ambitious program that required a highly complex integration between sellers and Amazon. com. It was clear to me that Amazon.com simply didn't have the human resources to manually govern a platform like this at scale. We had to make the third-party marketplace self-service. We had to provide a simple-to-use, highly intuitive tools for sellers as well as a system that would somehow cull sub-par sellers from the marketplace in order to keep customer trust high.

We quickly realized that the only way to accomplish all this was by taking a page from the OPW book. Fortunately, Jeff Bezos smiles upon projects designed to scale a business on a self-service platform. One of Jeff's favorite techniques is to create a *forcing function*—a set of guidelines, restrictions, or commitments that force a desirable outcome without having to manage all the details of making it happen. Forcing functions are a powerful technique used at Amazon.com to enforce a strategy or change.

One example of a forcing function was the concept of direct vs. indirect headcount. Direct headcount for a particular project would typically include system development engineers (SDE's), technical program managers, and people who negotiated contracts, such as vendor managers. In Jeff's mind, these were the essential skills to build a scalable company. All other headcount—all the people that don't directly create a better customer experience—was considered indirect. The forcing function was that acquiring direct headcount was relatively easy to get approved. However, indirect head count was constrained and had to be justified by demonstrating that it would decrease with scale in the business.

In building the third-party business, my indirect headcount consisted of the account managers I hired to help assist merchants complete their integration into Amazon.com. These account managers initially launched 15 to 20 merchants at a time, but before long they were launching 50 to 100 merchants. Eventually the number became astronomical. The forcing function did exactly what it was intended to do—it enabled us to build capabilities and processes that scaled well and became more efficient over time.

Under Clifford Cancelosi's direction, our team built tools, metrics, dashboards, alarms, and other capabilities to help the sellers meet all of their contractual commitments to us and to help them live up to our marketplace's high standards and ultimately, the expectations of their customers. We also built various technological and operational tools for monitoring their performance. For example, we policed the price and availability of an item on the seller's website to ensure it was not less expensive or easier to purchase than it was at the Amazon.com marketplace, and we flagged sellers who made unreasonable commitments or failed to keep their promises.

Eventually we built a seller's trust index based on all the touch points between merchant and customer as well as all the promises a merchant made. Every seller could track the answers to questions like, Is my content good? Am I fulfilling orders on time? Am I managing returns correctly? Is my customer feedback good? All of this was then rolled into an aggregated index yielding a score for each seller. We used many functions and algorithms to reward high-performing sellers—for example, by having them vault to the top of search results. In this way, the third-party marketplace evolved into a highly efficient, self-governing meritocracy. If a seller's score was really low, our management team would have various discussions with him before eventually removing him from the platform.

Equally important was Item Authority. Deceptively simple at first blush, Item Authority was perhaps the merchant program's quintessential invent-and-simplify innovation and a major reason for our success. In order to increase item selection, availability, and price competition, we signed up multiple sellers of the same items. Item Authority reconciled onto one page all of the various content from sellers selling the same item. This forced sellers to compete on price, selection, and convenience while markedly improving the customer experience. Instead of having to look through pages and pages for the best deal on a single item—which is essentially how eBay worked at the time—customers were presented with the most competitive offers all in one place.

Taken together, all these innovations worked remarkably well. Today, there are over two million third-party sellers at Amazon.com, accounting for 40 percent of all Amazon units shipped and sold. Here is how Amazon.com describes the mission and critical nature of Item Authority (the language comes from a job description):

> Item Authority is a mission-critical service at the heart of Amazon's business, and we are looking for a passionate, results-oriented, inventive software manager to head it up.
>
> When a merchant submits a product for listing in Amazon's catalog, Item Authority searches the catalog for matches. It either approves assigning that offer to a page, authorizes creation of a new page, or rejects the submission with an error. And it does this tens of millions of times per day.
>
> This "Matching" technology enables the creation of high quality Single Detail Pages (SDP) that help Amazon provide a great experience for our customers. It relies heavily on search technology (using A9), auto-classification, custom rules, and machine learning techniques for success. The ideal candidate thrives in a fast-paced environment, understands elements of matching, search,

and machine learning, and will help us build features that reduce merchant friction and drive revenue for Amazon.[3]

Described this way, it all sounds rather matter-of-fact, even obvious. But now that you know the story behind the story, you can see that inventing Item Authority and the other elements of Amazon's third-party seller program, and then simplifying them for the benefit of every user of the platform, was far from easy.

Fulfillment by Amazon

Many classic cases of invent and simplify at Amazon.com are behind-the-scenes processes and capabilities in fulfillment and customer service. One example is Fulfillment by Amazon (FBA), an idea driven by the success of the third-party seller business. Over the first decade of its existence, Amazon.com had built a vast system of physical storage space, technological systems, and processes that optimized item location in correlation with demand. As the third-party sellers' marketplace took off, it became clear that if we could allow others to leverage those capabilities, there would be a lot of upside for both our new third-party business and for Amazon.com as a whole.

The idea germinated when Amazon.com signed partnership agreements with Toys "R" Us and Target to run their e-commerce infrastructures. When both companies began storing their items in the Amazon fulfillment network, it became clear that our capabilities offered an opportunity to create increased economies of scale and utilization for Amazon.

The concept was remarkably simple: "You sell it, we ship it." With FBA, you store your products in Amazon.com's fulfillment centers, and Amazon workers pick, pack, ship, and provide customer service for these products. Amazon had created one of the most advanced fulfillment networks in the world, and any business could now benefit from their expertise. In a 2013 survey, 73 percent of respondents reported that their unit sales had increased on Amazon.com by more than 20 percent since joining FBA.[4]

In addition, products listed through FBA also became eligible for free Super Saver Shipping and Amazon Prime shipping discounts, gift wrapping, 24/7 Amazon customer service, and up-to-the-minute countdown for one-day shipping. In other words, sellers are able to piggyback on arguably the most powerful retail brand in the world. A great new flywheel!

In the 2011 shareholder letter, Jeff writes:

> Fulfillment by Amazon (FBA) shipped tens of millions of items on behalf of sellers. When sellers use FBA, their items become eligible for Amazon Prime, for Super Saver Shipping, and for Amazon returns processing and customer service. FBA is self-service and comes with an easy to use inventory management console as part of Amazon Seller Central. For the more technically inclined, it also comes with a set of API's so that you can use our global fulfillment center network like a giant computer peripheral.[5]

Amazon Web Services

No discussion of Amazon.com's platform businesses would be complete without some analysis of Amazon Web Services (AWS). It is a prime example of Jeff's "invent and simplify" principle. AWS offers companies technologies and capabilities that provide the ability to grow infrastructure instantaneously and to shrink it back if the need diminishes. This elasticity in resource usage gives companies momentum on a vast new scale.

Having built one of the world's largest infrastructures for e-commerce, Amazon.com was not content simply to leverage this new technology for its own business. Instead, it also became the leader and critical innovator in cloud computing, creating a business now estimated at around $3.8 billion in revenues (2013) that could be worth $19 billion to $30 billion if it were a standalone company.[6]

In his 2011 shareholder letter, Jeff writes:

> Amazon Web Services (AWS) has grown to have over thirty different services and thousands of large and small businesses and individual developers as customers. One of the first AWS offerings, the Simple Storage Service or S3, now holds over 900 billion data objects with over a billion being added every day. S3 routinely handles more than 50,000 transactions per second and has peaked at close to a million transactions per second. All AWS services are pay-as-you-go and radically transform capital expense into variable cost. AWS is self-service: you don't need to

negotiate a contract or engage a salesperson – you just read the online documentation and get started. AWS services are elastic – they easily scale up and easily scale down.[7]

You can see the pattern: the radical transformation of an industry aching for a new delivery model, in this case for cloud-based technology services; the development of a process for driving dramatically lower costs by providing self-service capabilities; and the drive toward scale as a platform business. (See Appendix A, "Future-Ready Self-Service," for a further explanation of why the concept of self-service is such a powerful value-creating strategy.)

Imitate the Competition, and Don't Be Afraid to Fail

In business, innovation is great—but it's clear that in many high-risk fields, mimicry pays off even better. Let the other guy originate the idea, invest the capital, discover a market, and develop operating processes. Then slide in, steal the blueprint, improve upon it, and scale it until the other guy has been left in the dust. The copycat often has a distinct advantage in this competition; the original innovator is typically emotionally bound to the original idea and hesitant to change it. The mimic has the benefit of an objective perspective and a willingness to course correct as needed.

Early on, Amazon.com tried to launch an auction business, but it couldn't out-auction eBay. Learning from our failure, we took the eBay concept and recast it with distinct Amazon.com values and technology, creating our ultra-successful third-party seller program. Jeff likes to say "Failure happens." Stumbles are a part of life, but at Amazon. com it is imperative that you learn something useful from them.

Don't be afraid to fail; some of the best ideas at Amazon have emerged from the ashes of defeat. But if you expect to have a long career at Amazon, make sure that failure doesn't happen a lot—regardless of how much you may learn in the process.

4. Leaders Are Right—A Lot

Leaders at Amazon are right—not always, but a lot. They have strong business judgment, and they spread that strong judgment to others through the utter clarity with which they define their goals and the metrics they use to measure success.

Make no mistake; there is a high degree of tolerance for failure at Amazon.com. A successful culture of innovation cannot exist without it. But what Jeff Bezos cannot tolerate is someone making the same mistake over and over again, or failing for the wrong reasons.

Therefore, leaders at Amazon are expected to be right far more often than they are wrong. And when they are wrong—which of course will happen when a company continually pushes the envelope, as Amazon does—they are expected to learn from their mistakes, develop specific insights into the reasons for those mistakes, and share those insights with the rest of the company.

The resulting culture of learning, growth, and accountability would be impossible without a high premium on *clarity*—clarity in the setting of goals, the communication of those goals throughout the organization, the establishment of metrics, and the use of those metrics in gauging the success or failure of any initiative. Practices like "fudging the numbers," "guesstimating," "approximating," and "bending the rules," as well as deadlines that aren't real deadlines and targets that are purely aspirational rather than firm objectives—all of these are anathema at Amazon.com.

As I've mentioned, one of the reasons I'm able to write out a description of Amazon's fourteen leadership secrets eight years after I left the company is the exceptionally clear way we articulated our goals and processes as a team and as an organization. Great leaders (like Jeff Bezos) develop a strong, clear framework; then they constantly apply that framework and articulate it accurately to their team. Get this right from the outset and you've got an excellent mechanism for scaling good decision-making from top to bottom.

Interestingly enough, as leaders at Amazon.com we were required to write out our ideas in a long, narrative form, which may seem contrary to the value of clarity. After all, don't most business presentations involve a series of bullet-point PowerPoint slides that are supposed to boil down complex concepts into a handful of brief, vivid phrases?

But at Amazon, PowerPoint slides were not allowed. If you needed to explain a new feature or investment to the S-Team or Jeff himself, you began by writing a five to seven page essay. After you finished that, you reviewed it and trimmed it down to maybe two pages of text for the executives. I can't tell you how many of my weekends were consumed by this writing and editing process. Then, at the beginning of the meeting, you would pass out this narrative and sit quietly for ten minutes while everyone read it.

The two-page document was a useful tool for sharing a set of ideas with your colleagues. But even more important was the process of working on the plan or proposal, describing it in a narrative so that important nuances, principles, and features were clear is a critical goal. As Dwight D. Eisenhower said, "Plans are nothing; planning is everything". Jeff believes that reliance on PowerPoint presentations dumbs down the conversation and does not push teams to think all the way through their topic. As he explained in a 2013 Charlie Rose interview, "When you have to write your ideas out in complete sentences and complete paragraphs, it forces a deeper clarity of thinking." By contrast, in the typical PowerPoint show, "You get very little information, you get bullet points. This is easy for the presenter, but difficult for the audience."[1] Written documents share more information without the need of additional explanation. When you have to be super specific, it further drives a culture of clarity, commitment, and accountability.

Jeff also believes that successful leaders, when presented with new evidence and data, are able to adapt their perspective. Accordingly, he looks for people who are constantly revising their understanding and circling back on problems they thought they'd already solved. He also looks for leaders who can maintain a remarkably granular understanding of their businesses through metrics, intensity, and great program execution. (It's a principle I will further explore in Chapter 12, "Dive Deep.") He believes that his system of corporate communication via written-out narratives will develop ideas much more effectively, deeply, and quickly than oversimplified bullet points and pie charts.

The Future Press Release

The style and format of Amazon.com project vision statements offers another excellent example of the narrative as a forcing function. Written as a short, simple, clear, digestible narrative, the Amazon "future press release" creates very little wiggle room and holds the highlighted team's feet to the fire by introducing specific parameters and deadlines that are expected to be met. So useful is this technique that an Amazon product launch almost always begins with what we used to call a *future press release*—an announcement of the product written before its development even began, used for internal purposes only. Crafting the future press release forced us to articulate for ourselves what would be newsworthy about the product at the very end of the development process.

This is a great way to define clear and lofty goals, requirements, and objectives, and to build broad understanding from the start of a program or enterprise change. Any time your organization is beginning to undertake a critical enterprise or competitive endeavor—launching a new product, undergoing a transformation, or entering a new market—writing a future press release is a great technique. Follow these rules to make them effective:

- Write the release as if you are writing at some future point in time where success has been achieved and realized. For example, when looking forward to the introduction of a new product, writing a press release as if at the day of product launch is good, but even better is a date sometime after launch, where true success can be discussed.
- Discuss why the initiative is important to customers or other key stakeholders. How did the customer experience improve? What benefits have customers received? Then discuss other reasons why it was important.

- Set audacious, clear, and measurable goals, including financial results, operating objectives, and market share.
- Outline the principles used that led to success. This is the trickiest and most important step. Describe the hard things accomplished, the important decisions along the way, and the design principles that led to success.

The future press release is a type of forcing function. It paints a clear vision to galvanize understanding and commitment. Once it has been reviewed and approved, teams have a difficult time backing out of the promises it implies. As the project continues, a leader can refer to the press release and use it to remind and hold teams accountable.

Here is the future press release we might have written in 2002 when launching the third-party selling business:

Amazon Announces Huge Growth in Third-Party Selling, Delighting Customers and Sellers

Seattle, WA: Amazon announced results for the third-party selling business today. Using the third-party selling platform, Amazon customers can now shop across many categories of products today including apparel, sporting goods, home decor, jewelry and electronics with incredible selection, price and an experience equaling orders fulfilled by Amazon.

"The Amazon customer now thinks about Amazon for any retail need, thanks to the third party selling business. Over 30% of all orders

at Amazon are now third party sold and fulfilled orders, across 10 new and expanded product categories," explained Director of Merchant
Integration John Rossman. "We tackled several
difficult hurdles to make this successful, with
the key being that sellers had a great experience.
Sellers can now register, list products to sell, take
orders and fulfill in the middle of the night, without ever having to talk to someone at Amazon."

If you want to increase your chances of achieving your
goals when launching any important initiative, make sure
you define and explain those goals with utter clarity from
the very beginning. The future press release is a useful tool
for making that happen.

Clarity and the Culture of Performance

There is no hiding from your failures in a culture that
holds people accountable for their metrics. As Manfred
Bluemel, a former senior market researcher at Amazon, once
said, "If you can stand a barrage of questions, then you have
picked the right metric. But you had better have your stuff
together. The best number wins."[2]
Bluemel was referring to Amazon.com's "gladiator culture." Because the numbers provide crystal-clear, incontro-
vertible proof of which leaders are right a lot, Amazon.com
operates to as close to a true meritocracy as possible. I cannot
overstate how important this is for minimizing bureaucracy in
the organization. When Jeff purchased *The Washington Post*
in 2013, a reporter at the paper interviewed me about this

cultural phenomenon at Amazon.com. I explained how key judgments were made during my years at the company: "It was not the title but rather who's got the best idea. Who's bringing the solution to the table? That's what was most important."[3]

To be blunt, as an Amazon.com leader, you don't get the chance to make a lot of mistakes. Screw up for long enough, or for the wrong reasons, and the island will simply vote you off. It is the strongest culture of performance I have ever experienced, and it is directly tied to metrics and results.

"Did I Have a Good Day Today?" The Engineer's Answer

At Amazon.com, having a balanced, well-engineered scorecard of metrics that is consistently reviewed day over day, week over week, provides deep insights into what works and what doesn't. It also places sole responsibility for success and failure on you as a leader.

Repeatable, consistent performance reflected in metrics is the gold standard for success at Amazon. Without access to a consistent set of metrics, an Amazon.com leader would be flying blind, and such risky behavior is not acceptable at the company. Amazon.com relies on real-time metrics or instrumentation more than any other company I have ever been involved with. Real data and real insights from the customer experience are used continually to answer the question, "Did I have a good day today?" If your metrics are in place, they are real-time, and your team and processes use them, this question yields a simple "yes" or "no" answer.

It takes foresight to do leadership-by-the-numbers correctly. You must embed real-time metrics from the very start of a program, because they are nearly impossible to retrofit.

The Amazon experience shows us that the single biggest opportunity for companies operating today is to completely rethink their concept of metrics. Most companies use what's called batch architecture to record large sets of transactions or other quantitative updates and to process them periodically (daily or weekly is typical). Batch architecture is very last century. In this day and age, you need real-time data, real-time monitoring, and real-time alarms when trouble is brewing—not lag-time metrics that hide the real issues for 24 hours or longer. Your business should operate like a nuclear reactor. If a problem arises, you need to be aware immediately.

This is why the word *instrumentation* is useful. It gives a different feel than *metrics* or *business intelligence*. An airplane pilot needs accurate real-time data. There can be no latency because there is no "down time" in a plane. Introducing the concept of instrumentation was a big and important change at Amazon.com, closely tied to our commitment to application programming interfaces (APIs) and service-oriented architectures (SOA). Instrumentation as a critical feature provided the dashboard to understand performance and issues in a real-time manner. In pursuit of true instrumentation, Amazon.com is constantly developing its real-time capabilities. During my time at the organization, Amazon.com tracked its performance against roughly 500 measurable goals, nearly 80 percent of which had to do with customer objectives.[4]

As I mentioned in Chapter 3, while I was heading up our third-party seller business, we decided we wanted the customers to have as much trust in buying from a third party as they did in buying from Amazon.com itself. Only because we embedded real-time instrumentation from the very outset could we ask a third-party seller, "Why aren't you fulfilling this on time?" or "Why is this item available at your site but not through Amazon.com?" The key is that our measurement tools had to be actionable and very current—as close to real-time as possible. We started with the concept of "perfect orders," already used in Amazon retail as a way of measuring seller performance. The specific metrics we developed to measure seller performance included:

Order defect rate (ODR). This is the percentage of a seller's orders that have received negative feedback (such as a one-star or two-star customer rating), an A-to-Z Guarantee claim, or a service credit card chargeback request (when a customer disputes a credit card charge with his or her bank). ODR allows Amazon.com to measure overall performance with a single metric. Obviously, a seller who maintains a high percentage of negative feedback is failing to live up to Amazon.com's customer-centric philosophy.[5]

Pre-fulfillment cancellation rate. This is the percentage of orders cancelled by a seller for any reason prior to shipment confirmation.

Late shipment rate. This is the percentage of orders with a shipment confirmation that is overdue by three or more days. Orders that are ship-confirmed late may lead to increased customer contacts and negatively impact customer experience.

Refund rate. This is the percentage of orders refunded by a seller for any reason.

All sellers should be working toward achieving and maintaining a level of customer service that meets the following performance targets:

- Order defect rate: < 1%
- Pre-fulfillment cancel rate: < 2.5%
- Late shipment rate: < 4%

Failure to meet these targets often results in the removal of the individual's selling privileges. Internally, seller metrics become bundled with even more measures of effectiveness and quality of seller performance, including customer ratings and the number of customer service contacts.[6]

Systems and software engineers will always be at the top of the food chain in a culture of innovation and metrics because they create the proprietary algorithms that enable leaders to have their fingers on the pulse of their businesses every second of the day. Jeff Bezos and Amazon have a deep belief that small teams of world-class engineers can out-innovate massive bureaucracies. Why? It has a lot to do with the instinctive preference for clarity that engineers develop through a lifetime of working with numbers and system requirements. Whereas bureaucrats automatically obfuscate, engineers automatically clarify. Clarification is the Amazon way, and is the basis for the culture of accountability that Jeff prides himself on creating.

5. Hire and Develop the Best

Leaders at Amazon raise the performance bar with every hire and promotion. They recognize exceptional talent, and willingly move them throughout the organization. Leaders develop leaders and take seriously their role in coaching others.

In 2009, Amazon.com acquired ecommerce footwear company Zappos.com for $807 million in Amazon.com stock, plus about $40 million in cash and restricted stock.[1] While many were shocked by the deal, it made perfect sense to me—though not for the reason given in Jeff Bezos's official statement, which read, "Zappos is a customer-focused company. We see great opportunities to learn from each other and create even better experiences for our customers." While that is true, the primary organic connection between the two firms lies in their hiring policies.

Zappos CEO Tony Hsieh has become the latest standard bearer for a successful CEO-driven company culture. He has been quoted as saying that hiring mistakes had cost his organization $100 million. In response, he implemented a fairly radical policy of paying new hires to quit. It's a strategy that's so counterintuitive yet so transparent in its thinking that I was immediately reminded of Jeff Bezos.

What's the thinking behind paying employees to quit? Pretty simple, really. It's about testing for commitment. If you're willing to take $2,000 to leave Zappos (which was the offer last time I checked), then you obviously haven't bought into what the company is trying to do. I don't know for sure, but I suspect that Hsieh's gutsy "all-in" requirement from his employees was a major driver in Jeff's decision to buy his company.

Jeff didn't offer me money to leave Amazon at any point during my tenure, but (as I've mentioned) I did endure 23 interviews over six weeks before being hired in the first place. I've heard others compare the process to the oral exam that a Ph.D. candidate must survive. I don't have a doctorate, but that sounds about right. The scrutiny is very, very intense. A typical interview day at Amazon can last nine hours. You may find yourself speaking to a group of people who will be working for you if you are hired. You may find yourself sitting in on a strategic meeting with company brass. You may be expected to contribute a solution to a real-time problem. You may even be shown the door before you ever get started. This is a test of commitment that is very comparable to Zappos's $2,000 exit offer and reflects the same belief in the crucial importance of hiring and retaining only the right people.

From the beginning, Jeff understood how important it was to seed Amazon with people who embodied the culture he wanted to create—that your people *are* your company. As a result, his standards are shockingly high. As Jeff often says, it's better to let the perfect person go than to hire the wrong person and have to deal with the ramifications. Why? Because it is a difficult, time-consuming, and expensive process to get rid of a bad hire—and in the meantime, they are dragging down those around them by their failure to help keep the flywheel of continuous growth and improvement humming at full strength.

Raising the Bar on Hiring

In the beginning, Jeff personally okayed every hire. After a few years, for obvious reasons, that became impossible to do. So in order to maintain his own high standards within the rapidly expanding organization, he created what he called the *bar raiser.*

The bar raiser is an individual appointed to serve as the last line of defense to ensure Jeff's standards of excellence. The bar raiser has veto power over any potential hire—regardless of the candidate's pedigree or his popularity among the rest of the hiring group. The bar raiser's job is to ensure that the next hire should increase the company's collective IQ, capacity, and capability—not decrease it. He or she also has to gauge how "fungible" the candidate is—that is, how capable of expanding into new roles and new areas of the business. Jeff famously put the philosophy this way: Five years after an employee was hired, he said, that employee should think, "I'm glad I got hired when I did, because I wouldn't get hired now."[2]

It's quite an honor to be named a bar raiser. The selection is based on the success and retention of the hires you've already made. Yet in having a veto over hiring, the role often puts you in direct opposition to the team doing the hiring. As an outside voice, your job is be an independent force, free from the pressure of work demands that sometimes lead hiring teams to make hasty or short-sighted decisions.

Even if you are not the bar raiser, your role in the hiring process is vital. Jeff would frequently tell us all that a hiring decision was probably the most important decision we could make as a member of the organization. We all knew that every successful candidate's career was inextricably linked to our own. And this was, without a doubt, the most effective forcing function for excellence.

Another was our custom recruiting application, which forced every interviewer to provide a lengthy, narrative analysis of the candidate and a yes-or-no recommendation (with no "maybe" option available). Your notes were expected to be detailed enough to justify your answer; the after-interview questioning could almost be as intense and consuming for the interviewer as it had been for the interviewee. The data was then immediately processed and applied to the next round of interviews. The process was so efficient that the next set of interviewers would often adapt their questions to push the candidate in directions suggested by answers they had provided just an hour or two earlier. As an interviewer, I sometimes forgot to listen to the candidate's answers because I was so busy directing my line of questioning to suit the previous interviewer's data or scribbling madly to record everything said.

After the interviews were completed, the hiring manager and bar raiser would review the notes and the votes of every interview. If a debrief was required, it was mandatory that everyone attend. And, of course the bar raiser could veto the hire without question, no matter how the team or hiring manager felt.

It was an absurdly rigorous process, one that would be considered wildly excessive at almost any other company. But if you really believe that your people *are* your company, why not invest the time and effort required to identify and hire only the very best?

Because standards are so high, hiring can be problematic. What many people don't realize is that Amazon.com almost went out of business in 2000, not long before I arrived. There was not enough revenue and way too much cost. The stock price plunged from $100 to $44 to $20 to below $5. The company closed down customer service, and massive layoffs ensued. Over the next few years, it was tremendously difficult to hire the best because we wouldn't pay them what they deserved and the stock options were far from enticing. There was a lot of risk and we basically expected people to take a pay cut to join us.

Yet the incredible commitment to hiring only the best remained unwavering. One colleague of mine wasn't able to find a suitable hire for over two months, so they just axed the position and told him that, if he hadn't been able to make the hire, then he obviously didn't need the person in the first place.

Of course, Amazon isn't above taking advantage of shortcut methods for identifying great talent. In a 2012 *CNN Money* article, Adam Lashinsky explained how Amazon. com had gone on a "military hiring spree" because Jeff was impressed with veterans' logistical know-how and bias for action.[3] In fact, Amazon.com has a dedicated military recruiting website and a highly consistent hiring and retention record for ex-military personnel.

This practice of hiring veterans isn't about expressing gratitude for ex-soldiers' service to our country. Veterans fit Jeff's business model. As a result, Amazon.com has not bothered to launch a huge PR campaign about its military employment program. Jeff just realized it was good business.

The Passing Grade Is A

The kiss of death at Amazon.com is being known as a "solid guy." While this might seem like a perfectly acceptable description at another company, Jeff's perception was different. As far as he was concerned, everyone at Amazon is fortunate to be there. People who didn't excel at their jobs were failing to contribute appropriately, in effect free-riding on the rest of us. As leaders, we were expected to work with laggards like these to improve their performance into the A+ category—or else find some way to incent these people to leave.

As a result, Amazon.com experienced systematic and significant turnover during my years there. Jeff told us to focus our positive reinforcement on our A+ people; he was comfortable with a high degree of churn below that standard.

This strategy was distinctly underlined by the compensation policy. At Amazon.com, the vast majority of stock options go to the A+ employees; only the crumbs go to the B and C players. And since the salaries were, relatively speaking, quite low (I think the top salary at the time was $155k), a vast majority of our compensation came in the form of stock. So being "a solid B" meant a significant falloff in stock options and promotion opportunities. It was all part of Jeff's way of instilling a sense of ownership in the company: our financial fortunes were directly tied to the success of the company.

Only seeking out, hiring, and retaining the very best people makes it possible to insist upon the highest standards of performance in the everyday activities of your company.

6. Insist on the Highest Standards

Leaders at Amazon set high standards—standards that many people consider unreasonably high. Leaders are continually raising the bar and driving their teams to deliver an ever-increasing level of quality. Leaders also ensure that the few defects that elude the quality process do not get sent down the line, and that problems are fixed so they stay fixed.

In earlier chapters of this book, I outlined numerous ways Jeff Bezos and the leadership team at Amazon.com have maintained "unreasonably high" standards of quality. The question is, how has such a large, complex organization managed to embed these standards into the DNA of the organization, from entry-level customer service representatives to the CEO himself? The answer begins with the seriousness and consistency with which the company applies its stated values—the Amazon leadership principles. Those principles are challenging—even inspiring—but also exacting in their demands.

Here's the most important thing about the principles: most of them refer to the expectations that Amazon has for leaders. (You've probably noticed that I've echoed that language in this book.) It sends a subtle but powerful message that empowers every Amazon.com employee to act and think like a leader. When everyone behaves like a leader, it acts as a forcing function for the relentlessly high standards that Jeff insists upon.

Jeff believed that his workforce, like his technology, should be constantly improving. He believed every new hire should improve the talent pool, just as every new technological process should improve efficiency and eliminate operational friction. And as the organization grew beyond the size where Jeff could personally enforce his high standards of performance, he developed instrumentation and metrics to play that role. One of these standards-enforcing tools is the *service level agreement*.

Service Level Agreements

A service level agreement (SLA) is a kind of contract that specifies the precise standards to which a particular service will be held. A well-written SLA will define the inputs, outputs, and the metrics that will be used to define acceptable quality and performance. At Amazon.com, SLAs are used to define expectations for the services provided to both external and internal customers.

Because bad customer experiences are simply not acceptable at Amazon.com, SLAs are written in such a way that the worst experiences are still very, very good compared to the rest of the industry. When you settle for the median, mediocrity sets in. That's where many companies get SLAs wrong.

Jeff relentlessly conveys to his team that even small service failures are far from trivial. For example, one of Amazon. com's metrics shows that even a minuscule 0.1-second delay in a webpage loading can translate into a 1 percent drop in customer activity. For that reason, the amazon SLA specifies that the worst page load time—experienced by customers no more than one tenth of one percent of the time—must be three seconds or less. These SLAs are heavily negotiated. Part of the weekly metrics review is discussing and understanding the root causes of SLA failures and the planned fixes. What's probably most impressive is that everything at Amazon.com has an SLA—everything. For instance, the time between an image's upload and the moment it appears on the website has an SLA. So does the time it takes to change a third party's inventory from ten to eight. If it can be measured, it is—and an exceptionally high standard of service is attached to it.

This dedication to real-time metrics and SLAs is one of the most unique aspects of Amazon.com. Most organizations don't have the ability to collect and manage this much near-real-time data. They don't have the ability to insist on SLA instrumentation and agreements or the investment mentality to make this happen. Doing so is not cheap—but at Amazon.com, instrumentation is a non-negotiable launch requirement for any new program.

As a result, Jeff and his leadership team always have a very clear picture of the organization's health. Needless to say, if your numbers don't reflect Jeff's expectations, you'll hear about it soon enough.

"Cookies or Cookies & Crumpets?"

In 2003, I was helping with the launch of a third-party store devoted to gourmet food. Amazon.com uses a hierarchy of "browse nodes" to organize its items for sale. Each node represents a category of items for sale rather than the items themselves—for example, Harry Potter books rather than an individual title from the J.K. Rowling book series. Browse node IDs are positive integers that uniquely identify product collections, such as Literature & Fiction (17), Medicine (13996), Mystery & Thrillers (18), Nonfiction (53), or Outdoors & Nature (290060). Amazon.com uses over 120,000 browse node IDs in the U.S. market alone.

Anyway, Jeff and the small group running the launch were having a conversation about the relevant browse nodes for the gourmet food store. It was one of those rare times when Jeff was in a really good mood. He was enjoying himself. Perhaps partly for this reason, we spent literally 20 minutes deeply discussing whether or not one browse node should be "Cookies" or "Cookies & Crumpets." A crumpet, Jeff argued, is actually a thick, flat savory cake, not a cookie, and thus deserved to be recognized as such.

The level of detail involved in this discussion bordered upon the absurd, but Jeff was entirely engaged and deadly serious about the decision's importance. To this day, whenever I am catch myself thinking that a decision is "not that important," I ask myself, "Cookies or Cookies & Crumpets?"

After reading this story you might think, "Jesus, what a micromanager! How does anything ever get done?" You'd have a point. Many of Jeff's standards *are* unreasonably high. And as a result, efficiency is occasionally sacrificed. In fact, some of the worst leaders I encountered at Amazon.com were the ones who hid behind ridiculous standard critiques. They became parrots of ideology, instead of being pragmatic in its application. Like any good idea or concept, the idea of high standards can be carried to a non-productive extreme.

Most of these bureaucratic parrots didn't last long, however. Because Amazon.com is a culture of metrics and performance, everything eventually comes out in the wash.

More than a few ex-Amazon.com employees have described the organization as a large company that functions like a start-up—meaning, I believe, that they feel as if they were required to do excellent work at a frenetic, breakneck pace while still adhering to time-consuming processes like the long-form written narrative and other elaborate communication processes.

This is all true, I suppose. But here's the thing. If you want to work for Jeff, you have to understand that the leadership principles are more than just nebulous guidelines. None of the 14 principles mentions the need for a healthy work-life balance. That is not an accident. Jeff expects all of his people to function as both owners and leaders. He wants you to drive the business as if it were your own car, not some weekend rental.

And the truth is that Jeff's maniacally high standards exist for a reason. There's a lot at stake when your entire storefront is a website. In 2012, the Amazon.com site went down for 49 minutes. A small glitch? Maybe. But as a result, the company lost sales of nearly $5.7 million.[2]

One of the original names for Amazon.com was Relentless.com.[3] Eventually this name was jettisoned because it had too many negative connotations, but that word lives on in Jeff's insistence on the highest standards. It takes a certain kind of personality to succeed in an organization like Amazon.com. As an employee, you really do have to adopt a long view, just like Jeff's, and truly believe you are part of something very big—something that is changing the world.

7. Think Big

Thinking small is a self-fulfilling prophecy. Leaders at Amazon create and communicate a bold direction that inspires results. They think differently and look around corners for big new ways to serve customers.

Jeff Bezos is closely associated with an organization called The Long Now, which is primarily made up of people concerned by society's ever-shortening attention span. On a Bezos-owned West Texas property they are building a clock that ticks once a year. The century hand advances once every 100 years, and the cuckoo will come out once every millennium for the next 10,000 years.[1]

Jeff is big on symbols. The 10,000-Year Clock is symbolic of his desire to always be thinking big and looking long-term—as a company, a culture, and a world. Bezos recognizes that "a lot of people believe that you should live for the now." He's not one of them. He recommends that people "think about the great expanse of time ahead of you and try to make sure that you're planning for that in a way that's going to leave you ultimately satisfied."[2]

I'm reminded of this quotation whenever I read about Jeff's quest to salvage one of Apollo 11's F-1 engines from the bottom of the Atlantic Ocean. I'm just extrapolating here, but I imagine he might consider the NASA space program—once the very definition of thinking big—as having lost its drive to really achieve anything as monumental as going to the moon. For him, dredging this symbol up from obscurity is a great metaphor for a renewed quest for greatness—a call to the American people to once again think big.

Or maybe he's just really into space stuff. I don't know.

Either way, it's clear that Jeff's emphasis of thinking big applies most of all to himself. You and I might consider Jeff a legend of entrepreneurial achievement and one of the greatest success stories in modern history. But in his mind, he still has a long way to go. He's openly said that he hasn't yet built "a lasting company" and that "the Internet in general and Amazon.com in particular, are still in Day One." Jeff is out to not just sell history books, but to also rewrite them. And if you want a seat on his bus, be prepared to "go big or go home."

A colleague told me this story about one S-Team meeting in 2002 when they were discussing the selection of merchandise Amazon would make available to customers. Chief information officer and senior vice president Rick Dalzell asked Jeff when "enough would be enough." Jeff responded, "When a factory in Paraguay can buy a railroad boxcar full of bauxite from a mine in China and transact it over Amazon, then we *might* be done."

After a moment, Dalzell asked if we would ever sell bull semen. Jeff said, "Well, why not? There is lots of margin in it." Then he turned to Jeff Wilke, the senior vice president of consumer business and said, "You *will* need refrigeration."

This story illustrates that there is probably nothing "too big" in the Amazon.com universe and why "think big" gets imbedded into everyone's behavior.

Leaders create and communicate a bold direction that inspires results. As I've explained, my challenge was to design and operate a capability that would allow third parties to sell at Amazon—not for 10 or 100 users but for tens of thousands. With that kind of scale in mind from day one, based on a vision that is massive, you're willing to invest in a way that you wouldn't with a modest vision of incremental change. This is one of Amazon's secret sauces—to think about the vast potential of a project from day one and create an inspired team that owns that.

Free Cash Flow—The Secret of Thinking Big

In his April, 2013, letter to shareholders, Bezos addressed one of the most important factors in Amazon.com's massive success—the willingness to sacrifice this year's profits to invest in long-term customer loyalty and product opportunities that will create bigger profits next year and for years thereafter.[3] Writer and former Wall Street analyst Henry Blodget responded to Jeff's letter in an April 14, 2013 *Business Insider* article that contrasted his long view with the myopic focus on today's bottom line that characterizes most companies. Blodget observed:

> This obsession with short-term profits has helped produce the unhealthy and destabilizing situation that now afflicts the U.S. economy: The profit margins of America's corporations are now higher than they ever have been in history, while the employee wages paid by America's corporations are the lowest they have ever been in history.

Meanwhile, a smaller percentage of America's adults are working than at any time since the late 1970s.[4]

Amazon.com has never put short-term profits ahead of long-term investment and value creation—a strategy many believe has the potential to boost the entire American economy. Sometimes overlooked is the fact that maintaining low margins—and deliberately eschewing short-term profits—is a brilliant strategy in the tumultuous age of the Internet. Not only do low prices drive customer loyalty, but they also discourage competition. If you want to jump into the fray against Amazon.com, you can't just match them on value—you have to significantly beat them. But that's easier said than done. Jeff has left very little room to huddle beneath Amazon.com's price umbrella, leaving most competitors out in the soaking rain.

"We've done price elasticity studies," Bezos once said. "And the answer is always that we should raise prices. We don't do that, because we believe—and we have to take this as an article of faith—that by keeping our prices very, very low, we earn trust with customers over time, and that actually does maximize free cash flow over the long term."[5]

Free cash flow is the key phrase in that comment. Jeff returned to the subject in a January 3, 2013, *Harvard Business Review* interview: "Percentage margins are not one of the things we are seeking to optimize. It's the absolute dollar free cash flow per share that you want to maximize. If you can do that by lowering margins, we would do that. Free cash flow, that's something investors can spend."[6]

The move towards free cash flow (FCF) as the primary financial measure at Amazon.com began in earnest when

Warren Jenson became CFO in October, 1999. That's the time when the finance organization began to move away from a percentage margin focus to a cash margin focus. Jeff loves to give his loud, guffaw laugh and toss out the axiom "Percentages don't pay the light bill—cash does!" He then follows up with the question, "Do you want to be a $200 million company with a 20 percent margin or a $10 billion company with a 5 percent margin? I know which one I want to be!" Again, the guffaw.

As explained in his 2004 letter to stockholders, Jeff likes the FCF model because it gives a more accurate view of actual cash generated through Amazon.com's operations (primarily retail sales) that is truly free to use in doing a number of things.[7] In the model Amazon.com uses, capital expenditures are subtracted from gross cash flow. This means that the cash is available to grow the business by adding new categories, creating new businesses, scaling through technology (done often and well at Amazon.com), or paying down debt (in 2004, Amazon.com had $4 billion and some FCF was used to pare that down). Of course, that extra cash could also be given back to stockholders in the form of dividends (never really considered) or given back to shareholders via stock repurchases (maybe someday—no, not really).

Jeff believed then, as he does now, that without constant innovation a company will stagnate. And the primary ingredient for investment in innovation is FCF.

This philosophy and the need to practice it successfully drove the creation of other capabilities, such as Amazon's robust, extremely accurate unit economic model. This tool allows folks like the merchants, finance analysts, and optimization modelers (known at Amazon.com as quant-heads) to understand how different buying decisions, process flows, fulfillment paths, and demand scenarios would affect a product's contribution profit. This, in turn, gives Amazon.com the ability to understand how changes in these variables would impact FCF. Very few retailers have this in-depth financial view of their products; thus, they have a difficult job making decisions and building processes that optimize the economics. Amazon.com uses this knowledge to do things like determine the number of warehouses they need and where they should be placed, quickly assess and respond to vendor offers, accurately measure inventory margin health, calculate to the penny the cost of holding a unit of inventory over a specified period of time, and much more.

While Amazon.com's short-term investors may grouse that Amazon.com should be "making more money," Jeff continues to build one of the most dominant, enduring, and valuable enterprises in the world. Meanwhile, other Internet boom companies have bit the dust, mostly because they put too much emphasis on short-term profitability and failed to invest enough in long-term value creation.

Jeff explains it this way, "Take a long-term view, and the interests of customers and shareholders align."[8] That's the philosophy that has made Amazon so successful. Another way of saying it: If you're inefficient and have fat margins, you die a Darwinian death.

On the Origin of Species . . . now there's a business model that thinks big.

The Regret Minimization Framework

One of my favorite Jeff concepts is the idea of the *regret minimization framework*. It was something he referred to every once in a while, especially when we were thinking big and preparing to do something that everyone thought was crazy . . . launching the third-party seller division, for instance.

Apparently, when Jeff decided he was going to quit his job and start a company that sold books online, his boss at D. E. Shaw advised him to think about it for 48 hours before making a final decision. So Jeff sat down and tried to find the right framework in which to make that kind of big decision. In typical Jeff Bezos long-term thinking manner, he referenced something he called his regret minimization framework. As he explained in a 2001 interview:

> I wanted to project myself forward to age 80 and say, "Okay, now I'm looking back on my life. I want to have minimized the number of regrets I have." I knew that when I was 80 I was not going to regret having tried this. I was not going to regret trying to participate in this thing called the Internet that I thought was going to be a really big deal. I knew that if I failed I wouldn't regret that, but I knew the one thing I might regret is not ever having tried. I knew that that would haunt me every day, and so, when I thought about it that way it was an incredibly easy decision. And, I think that's very good. If you can project yourself out to age 80 and sort of think, "What will I think at that time?" It gets you away from some of the daily pieces of confusion. You know, I left this Wall Street firm in the middle of the year. When you do that, you walk away from your annual bonus. That's the

kind of thing that in the short-term can confuse you, but if you think about the long-term then you can really make good life decisions that you won't regret later.[9]

This is advice that works well when applied to a personal career decision. But it works just as well when making a decision about the future of your business. Which choice will look best when you consider it, not six months or one year from now, but decades in the future? Chances are that's the right option—the one that holds out the promise of doing really big things.

8. Have a Bias for Action

Leader at Amazon value calculated risk taking. Speed matters in business. Many decisions and actions are reversible and do not need extensive study. So when you are in doubt, try something—and take advantage of the opportunities that being the first in the field can offer.

The physics of inertia show us that a body at rest has a tendency to remain at rest. In his book, *The Wall Street Journal Essential Guide to Management*, Alan Murray points out that a corollary of that physical principle is this: It's usually easier to stop things from happening than it is to make them happen.[1]

At Amazon.com, there is a natural tendency to push forward at all times. The right kind of person for Amazon. com is somebody who is astute and contemplative yet avoids paralysis from analysis—the kind of person who is always moving forward on things without waiting to be asked to do so. This is one of the best aspects of working at Amazon. com. There is no status quo—just a continual effort to push ahead. I read somewhere that Hall of Fame NFL coach Bill Parcells posted a sign in his locker room that read "Blame Nobody. Expect Nothing. Do Something." He would make an excellent leader at Amazon.com.

Jeff has always reassured his people that they will never be punished for erring on the side of action. This has resulted in both huge wins (the creation of one-click shopping) and colossal failures (the creation of Amazon Auction). There's a common assumption that it's important to know the exact right action to take before doing anything. That's not how things are viewed at Amazon. As Jeff once said, "If you never want to be criticized, for goodness' sake, don't do anything new."[2] (Of course, this bias for action and willingness to be wrong doesn't mean you can also be wrong repeatedly. Unlike Thomas Edison, leaders at Amazon don't get 2,000 tries at developing just the right filament for the light bulb.)

Sometimes the Mere Threat of a Big Idea Is Enough

In a December 1, 2013, television interview with Charlie Rose, Jeff sent the media into a tizzy by unveiling his plan to eventually use drones to facilitate same-day delivery of packages. While he admitted that this service was still some way off in the future and faced such obstacles as FAA regulations and limitations on package size, the drone story was great PR copy that was timed perfectly—the day before Cyber Monday, when reporters everywhere are focused on the retail industry. And it worked. Sales shot through the roof the morning after the interview aired, partly because Jeff's sly smile and the Amazon.com brand seemed to be plastered across every news media page and Internet blog.

The primary message I took from the interview was a simple one: Jeff's focus on the long view and on thinking big has clearly remained unchanged. If you are not inventing for your customers and improving their experience every day—even in ways that may hurt short-term financial results—then someone else will.

Even if drones never deliver a single package for Amazon, they make a highly effective symbol of Amazon.com's commitment to continuing to invent and simplify on fulfillment. As radical and controversial as drone delivery may seem today, the idea is perfectly in line with this strategy. And quite frankly, I wouldn't be shocked if Jeff finds a way to make them work.

Don't Let Simple Things Be Hard Things

A bias for action does have its down side. Many current and ex-employees at Amazon.com—especially in the early days—complained to me that they were occasionally not given the resources they needed to build things properly. There is continuous pressure to get things done as quickly as possible, which sometimes leads people to apply Band-Aids to problems rather than address the underlying issues. Some say Amazon would be better served by slowing down and moving at a more deliberate pace.

In response, Jeff would probably say, "If you double the number of experiments you do per year, you're going to double your inventiveness."[3] You may or may not agree with this philosophy, but it's hard to argue with it when Jeff propounds it—because he's proven it works.

Nonetheless, it is true that a bias for action tends to encourage decision-making that is based on gut instinct. There's a reason why a bias for action is often mentioned as a characteristic trait of successful start-ups. The time and money budgets of start-up companies simply don't allow for elaborate market analysis. And it's clear that Jeff has often followed his gut instincts over the years. He respects leaders who are willing to do the same.

However, this can cause a leader to run head-on into a paradox. Amazon.com has what I would call a *two-strike culture*. Leaders are expected to be right—a lot. They are encouraged to take risks, but they must be calculated risks. And a leader cannot completely blow it very often before being shown the door.

So how do you successfully balance a bias for action with the ability to be right a lot? By developing and monitoring the metrics. As Jeff likes to say, "Don't let simple things be hard things." Innovating products, increasing sales, recruiting great talent . . . these are hard things to do. Administrative and procedural tasks like collections should be simple. So a question like "Are we up to date on collections or not?" should be easy to answer. But at many companies, the information to answer questions like these is simply not available.

That's where the metrics come in. Creating an operational environment that automates processes and makes them clear and transparent allows you to invest more time and energy on the thornier issues that require more work and creativity.

So one of the keys to creating and sustaining a successful bias for action is having the right data in front of you at the right time. Of course, you have to trust that the data are trustworthy and accurate, and that's why Jeff puts so much stock into hiring the world-class engineers.

The seriousness of Jeff's commitment to the bias for action is shown by the thought he has given to rewarding and honoring it. For example, Amazon.com's system of iconography rewards and engages employees who develop new skills or attributes. These "merit badges" take the form of highly visible icons on their phone tool, the internal phone directory on the intranet of Amazon. You'd be surprised how effective this is at motivating people to take on new challenges.

Then there's the Just Do It award, which is presented at the quarterly all-hands meeting to employees who exemplify the values of a bias for action, ownership, frugality, and self-starting. The award may just be an old tennis shoe that's been mounted and bronzed, but it's also a highly coveted, very visible icon that winners display proudly in their offices.

Leaders understand that 100 percent certainty about the prospects for any new venture is almost never available. No matter how much research and analysis you do, the future can never be guaranteed. That's why Amazon rewards leaders who just do it—who respond to uncertainty by taking a (smart) risk and learning from the results.

9. Practice Frugality

A leader at Amazon tries not to spend money on things that don't matter to customers. Frugality breeds resourcefulness, self-sufficiency, and invention. No extra points are awarded for headcount or budget size.

Amazon.com has always been tremendously deliberate about keeping a cost- conscious, even cheap culture. Jeff firmly believes that frugality drives innovation. It is one of his favorite forcing functions. As he puts it, "One of the only ways to get out of a tight box is to invent your way out."[1] Every dollar saved is another opportunity to invest in the business. Eliminating cost structure from the business drives low prices, which drives the virtuous cycle flywheel.

When I was at Amazon.com, nobody flew first class. Everybody stayed in budget hotels. The company didn't pay for anybody's cell phone bill. Most important, this low-cost culture was executed consistently from top to bottom. Jeff drove the same little Honda for years after he founded Amazon.com. Perhaps most extraordinarily, Jeff's salary is $81,840—just $14,000 more than the average Facebook intern makes.[2]

Just as he did in 1997, Jeff fundamentally believes that Amazon is still in day one, and so he runs it with the cost-minded discipline normally applied to a brand new start-up. More than anything else, he fears and loathes complacency—especially since the company still operates on razor-thin profit margins, relying on high and growing volume to pay the bills. Keeping costs down is one way of fending off complacency. It also discourages employees from measuring their importance by the amount of money they spend. No extra points are awarded for headcount or budget size. Empire-building by managers is virtually impossible, in partly because there's just no money for it.

The Legend of the Door Desk

From the beginning, Jeff was adamant that Amazon was not going to create offices with big, elaborate desks. He figured all anyone needed was a place to work—and that included senior leadership as well. Early on in the company's history, someone came up with the idea of hammering legs on to doors to create more desks. Eventually, the "door desk" became Jeff's symbol for the low-cost, egalitarian culture he was trying to create. In fact, the company still hands out the Door Desk Award, a title given to select employees who have a "well-built idea" that creates significant savings for the company and enables lower prices for customers.

Ironically the door desk, one of Jeff's supremely effective symbols for company frugality, later became a symbol of mindless bureaucracy that nearly gave him a conniption fit. I found out about it at an all-hands meeting where Jeff was ranting about bureaucracy. What had set him off? Apparently someone had shipped door desks to our London office. "You know you're becoming a bureaucracy when you decide to spend money to ship [expletive] symbols to Europe!" he yelled.

I'm fairly certain someone lost their job over that one.

That hasn't stopped Jeff from searching for opportunities to create fresh symbols of frugality. For example, at the company's annual shareholders meeting in 2009, Bezos revealed that all the light bulbs had been taken out of the cafeteria vending machines. "Every vending machine has light bulbs in it to make the advertisement more attractive," Jeff explained. "So they went around to all of our fulfillment centers and took all the light bulbs out."[3] Amazon.com estimated that the measure saved tens of thousands a year on electricity. Not a huge sum in itself, but the gesture speaks volumes about the way this multi-billion-dollar company thinks.

No More Free Advil

Like any goal or policy, a good idea can go too far. Frugality can have a downside when it sends a message of not caring to employees or customers. Just visit Glassdoor. com, the website dedicated to employee comments about the companies they work for, and read about how many Amazon ex-employees cite the company's cheapness as the number one reason they jumped ship. Many people have warned that Amazon.com's policy of hiring temporary-contract workers could lead to low-quality work and inconsistent productivity, and waste resources on extra training.

Amazon.com has also been criticized for outsourcing its customer chat support to India. In one particular instance, an American customer went so far as to post the transcript of his wildly dysfunctional discussion with an Amazon.com chat support representative named "Farah," a woman who clearly had a tenuous relationship with the English language.[5] While this is hardly an uncommon problem in customer service among many U.S. companies, critics pointed to the unfortunate interaction as a sign that Amazon.com was growing too big to adhere to its stated principles.

To my mind, the fact that this story made the pages of *Business Insider* suggests that Amazon.com is still the gold standard when it comes to high customer service standards. But it also suggests that Amazon's quest for cost reduction carries with it the risk of compromising those standards—a challenge I'm sure Jeff Bezos is focusing on.

In *The Everything Store*, Brad Stone writes about how employees are impacted by the emphasis on frugality:

> Parking at the company's offices in South Lake Union costs $220 a month, and Amazon reimburses employees—for $180. Conference room tables are a collection of blond-wood door desks shoved together side by side. The vending machines take credit cards, and food in the company cafeterias is not subsidized. New hires get a backpack with a power adapter, a laptop dock, and orientation materials. When they resign, they're asked to hand in all that equipment—including the backpack.[4]

Stone goes on to report that, in the late 1990's, a newly installed executive "cut a rare office perk, free Advil, which he viewed as an unnecessary expense." The move set off "a near insurrection among employees," but was upheld.

All of that said, it's probably important to note that Amazon.com has industry-typical health insurance and dental plans, as well as its yearly employee stock grants and matching 401k program. The company pays enough to attract quality talent—but not enough to make people fat and happy, or to create the country-club atmosphere Jeff is trying to avoid. It's a delicate balance to strike for both customers and employees.

10. Be Vocally Self-Critical

Leaders at Amazon do not consider themselves, or their teams, above criticism. They benchmark themselves against the best, and they are proactive about revealing problems or mistakes, even when doing so is awkward or embarrassing.

Problems exist in every business. As every recovering alcoholic knows, the first step in fixing any problem is admitting that it exists. While many business teams and their leaders fool themselves by denying the existence of problems for weeks, months, and even years on end, Amazon. com leaders are expected to be intellectually honest. They acknowledge their shortcomings and continually ask, "How can we get better?"

Needless to say, the experience can be humiliating. As you may have gathered, Jeff Bezos is not always the most gentle and understanding of leaders. Knowing that you could be facing an experience only slightly less embarrassing than a public pillory, it's tempting to give the appearance that you or your team are progressing more quickly than you actually are, especially when reporting directly to Jeff. It's also tempting to remain quiet while others are telling a rosy story or making promises that you know are unlikely to be fulfilled. But a leader at Amazon.com is expected to speak up and make sure the truth is heard. After all, the alternative—hiding a problem and having it discovered down the road—is a terminable offense. Besides, when you tell the truth despite the pain it may cause, you encourage others to give you honest feedback, thereby preempting the need for others to criticize you.

For all these reasons, a leader at Amazon has to be willing to "open his kimono" and take responsibility for his mistakes. There simply is no other way.

The Journey and the End Results

In an interview on the Amazon Fulfillment website, Director of Fulfillment Miriam Park is asked which Amazon.com leadership principle resonates most with her. She answers, "Being vocally self-critical. I am humbled by the caliber of talent at Amazon and our willingness as leaders to acknowledge and learn from our mistakes. We value both the journey and the end results."[1]

Miriam understands Jeff's ethos precisely. In terms of the big picture, he surely cares about the end results—but he's also very much engaged in the journey. The end result is all about victory—overcoming competition, attracting and delighting millions of customers, enjoying rewards and acclaim. But the journey is about the struggle—the hard work, experiments, mistakes, reboots, and countless details that must be dealt with along the way to victory. Thinking about the ultimate victory may feed our egos, but we can't survive the journey without a large dose of authentic humility.

The principle of being vocally self-critical is one of the tools Jeff uses to help Amazon combat the danger of arrogance; the virus that has taken down countless hugely successful organizations. Jim Collins has done a wonderful job of illustrating how organizational decline is largely self-inflicted, specifically in his book *How the Mighty Fall.* He uses the ancient Greek term "hubris"—the excessive pride that destroys a hero—to describe how leaders become arrogant about their success and begin to view it as an entitlement. As a result, they lose sight of what caused their success in the first place.[2]

You may also recall from another classic Jim Collins book, *Good to Great,* that one of the keys to organizational greatness is the presence of Level 5 Leaders–leaders who blend humility and will. Collins says, "Like inquisitive scientists, the best corporate leaders we've researched remain students of their work, relentlessly asking questions–why, why, why?–and have an incurable compulsion to vacuum the brains of people they meet."[3]

Amazon.com expects everyone to be a Level 5 leader.

Which Dog Is Not Barking?

A vital corollary of humility and self-criticism is the readiness to recognize potential threats wherever they may be. No business is so powerful and successful that it can afford to overlook emerging competitors—even those that may appear innocuous or beneficent.

In the Sir Arthur Conan Doyle story "Silver Blaze," the legendary detective Sherlock Holmes must solve the mystery of a missing racehorse and the apparent midnight murder of its trainer. He eventually deduces that the crime was an inside job because the dog at the scene of the crime did *not* bark—indicating that the criminal was someone well known to the animal. Jeff likes to use this story of "the curious incident of the dog in the night-time" as a departure point for a discussion about the urgent need for leaders to critically address Amazon's blind spots as a company.

Clifford Cancelosi told me about how, at a Merchant Services leadership offsite meeting, one of Amazon's senior leaders recounted how the S-team had used the dog-not-barking exercise to recognize that one of the company's most significant long-term threats was none other than Google. On the surface, Google didn't seem like a direct competitor. In fact, they seemed like friends and potential allies. But as company leaders discussed Google's capabilities and some of the innovative products and services they'd been developing, they realized that Google had a growing capacity to migrate into Amazon's space. The exercise of looking for the "unbarking" dog helped reveal the possibility that a significant competitive threat was lurking right under their noses—invisible in plain sight.

In response, Amazon reduced its dependency on Google by improving its own search capabilities and creating places on the Web where customers could get to Amazon directly without Google.

The willingness to engage in constant self-examination—both as individual leaders and as an organization—is vital to maintaining success. And you can't conduct such self-examination effectively without a large dose of humility, and a willingness to look in the mirror and recognize honestly what you see there. In most organizations, the typical mentality is "I have so many obvious needs and threats, I can't possibly spend time looking for the non-obvious threats—much less doing something about them." Through these types of exercises, teams at Amazon can pick a couple of ideas, build programs around them, and make progress. These efforts often yield new innovations and other benefits, but only because maintaining healthy paranoia and always looking for improvement is a priority and a leadership value.

11. Earn the Trust of Others

Leaders at Amazon are sincerely open-minded, genuinely listen, and examine their own strongest convictions with humility. Their openness enables them to trust those around them—and to earn the trust of others in turn.

I've already talked about how important it is for the customer to trust the company. Amazon devotes itself single-mindedly to earning the customer's trust every day. But equally important is trust within the business—which means that leaders at Amazon must learn both to trust their colleagues and to earn their trust through transparency, commitment, and mutual respect. For many people, learning to do this isn't easy.

When I first arrived at Amazon.com, I felt exposed and vulnerable. I worried that I might be fired at any time because the standards and the stakes were so high. As a result, I insisted on personally handling too much of my team's work, feeling too anxious and untrusting to delegate enough to my colleagues.

Of course, I quickly learned that overloading myself was a recipe for disaster—I simply didn't have the time, energy, or skill to do everything well. I also wasn't sufficiently developing my people; I was hurting the organization by not training the leaders of the future, which is a cardinal sin at Amazon.com. I simply had to learn to trust.

Flourishing companies are filled with really bright people who have the authority to achieve, but also the confidence that, if they fail, someone will be there to pick them up off the floor, dust them off, and give them another shot. Amazon is such a company. One reason I really enjoyed my time there was the ability to work collaboratively without worrying about titles, organization charts, and official roles. All of those things got ditched at the door so that we could devote our energies to attacking problems. This is very different than at most organizations, where teams and individuals waste time playing a game of chicken, pointing fingers and trying to seize political advantages from one another.

Six Keys to Earning Trust

True collaboration is only possible in an atmosphere of trust. And that atmosphere is always set by a leader who has earned his team members' trust and who trusts them in return.

Unfortunately, almost everyone has had a boss at some time that simply didn't deserve to be trusted. He may have been gifted with MENSA-level intelligence and the charisma of George Clooney, but you were always waiting for the blaming, the backtracking, and the backstabbing to begin.

Jeff understands that a lack of trust perpetuates fear. If you fail to earn the trust of your team members, fear eventually becomes their primary driver. They will fear your opinions. They will fear your decisions and evaluations. They will fear failure. They will fear you. Once fear becomes dominant, the organization can barely operate, let alone be vocally self-critical.

Fortunately, there are proven ways to earn the trust of others. Here are six I have adapted from the blog of intentional leadership guru Michael Hyatt:

- *Open your kimono.* Learn to take accountability and admit faults—not recklessly or in a way that lets people exploit you, but rather in a way that demonstrates honesty and pursuit of improvement. Be willing to admit your own failures. If you put up a wall around yourself, your team will, too.

- *Take the hit.* When bad thing happen, resist the temptation to point the finger. As leader of a team, you need to accept responsibility for both the good and the bad. When your team members see that you are willing to take the blame even for mistakes that are not directly your fault, they will start to let go of fear and begin to trust you.

- *Build up your team members.* This is the opposite of taking the hit. Whenever appropriate, make sure you praise your team members in front of their peers and superiors. Never try to take sole credit for something good that your team did.

- *Ditch the leash.* Allow your team members freedom to explore new ideas and to be creative. If people feel that you are micro-managing them, they will stop trusting you. Make room for failure and, more importantly, the opportunity to learn from failure.

- *Accept confrontation.* Fighting is not good, but neither is false agreement. When there is a difference of opinion, promote open discussion. Explore solutions with the intent to solve problems. If disagreement never occurs, it's a warning sign that your team is afraid of telling you the truth.

- *Find the value in each person.* We all have weaknesses, but we also have strengths. Everyone brings something different to the table. Find what is unique in each individual and use that unique strength for the good of the team.[1]

Trust and the Two-Pizza Team

In his 2011 shareholder letter, titled "The Power of Invention," Jeff Bezos wrote, "Invention comes in many forms and at many scales. The most radical and transformative of inventions are often those that empower others to unleash their creativity—to pursue their dreams."[2]

Jeff was talking specifically about the ability of the platform business as a tool for empowering people, but I think the same description applies to trust in the workplace. Trust is the platform to truly empower your team.

Much has been written about Amazon.com's famous Two-Pizza Teams—working groups whose size is limited to six to ten individuals—the number of people that can be fed by an order of two pizzas. However, most people miss the point. What truly matters isn't team size—it's autonomy and accountability. The Two-Pizza Team is about trusting a small faction within an organization to operate independently and with agility.

At Amazon, Two-Pizza Teams work like little entrepreneurial hot houses. Insulated from the greater organization's bureaucracy, the Two-Pizza Teams encourage ambitious young leaders, provide opportunity, and instill a sense of ownership.

Should every organization in the world start authorizing the creation of Two-Pizza Teams to tackle its problems and creative challenges? No, because not every organization has the underlying culture of trust needed to make autonomous teams work effectively. If you work in a company that is dominated by fear, start trying to turn that atmosphere around. Once trust begins to flourish, creativity and innovation can flourish as well.

Just search the web for "2 pizza team lead" and you will find great references and examples of what a two-pizza team does.

12. Dive Deep

Leaders at Amazon operate at all levels, stay connected to the details, and audit them frequently. No task is beneath them, because they know that only a deep dive into the nuts and bolts of a process can really uncover opportunities and solve problems before they become insurmountable.

At Amazon.com, ownership means accountability. The leader is responsible for the entire lifecycle of a project or transaction and for all its possible outcomes. If you are a leader, you must be willing to go beyond the parameters of your job to improve the customer experience.

The corollary is that leaders understand details and metrics two to three degrees deeper than senior executives at most companies. They are keenly aware of their dependencies and therefore can discuss the details of any given project under their jurisdiction.

One driver of the dive-deep philosophy is the pure, relentless sense of curiosity that Jeff Bezos exemplifies and that he encourages among all those who work for him.

It's been widely reported that Jeff spends time working in Amazon.com's fulfillment centers. This is not just an excellent PR ploy; in fact, Jeff does not generally invite the media to join him on these trips. Jeff likes working alongside the hourly employees because he's curious about what they have to say and wants to see for himself precisely how efficient the process of fulfilling orders is.

Jeff's relentlessly inquisitive mind is one of his most prominent and distinctive features—and he demands the same from his people. As a result, experiments are encouraged, but the results must be rigorously measured. This combination of free thinking and disciplined analysis is very productive and makes diving deep a daily reality at Amazon.

The dive-deep philosophy is also driven by Jeff's awareness that a company is very much like an ecosystem. It is complex, constantly evolving, and thrives on diversity. This means that numerous possibilities for failure are continually emerging.

For this reason, as any major initiative unfolds at Amazon. com, Jeff stays as close to the project team and its data as he can, not only monitoring it but questioning it, poking holes in it, and examining every facet down to the smallest detail. Every leader in the company is expected to behave the same way. Every manager is expected to maintain a strong presence throughout a project's implementation, making continuous deep dives into the data, the processes, and the performance of every team member. It's a practice that enables every leader at Amazon.com to overcome traditional organizational barriers—another form of bureaucracy busting that crashes through the obstacles that might delay or distort progress or learning along the new performance dimensions. Leaders who are constantly digging deep into a challenge—*curious* leaders—dismantle silos and bureaucracy.

Of course, to dive deep, you need metrics and systems designed to collect and analyze them accurately, consistently and quickly. Leaders must have a willingness to dive deep, but Amazon.com's remarkable culture of metrics provides the data that rewards the effort. As SVP of Consumer Business Jeff Wilkie once said, "Math decisions always trump opinion and judgment. Most corporations make judgment-based decisions when data-based could be made."[1]

The desire to dive deep is also why (as I discussed in chapter 4) Jeff has banned PowerPoint and demands clear decision-making narratives. Putting together a slideshow makes it all too easy for employees to only skim the surface of their ideas while creating the illusion of an intelligent argument. On the other hand, knowing they must publicly present an in-depth essay to their peers and their boss forces them to dive in a little deeper. It helps creates an atmosphere of accountability because it means that you have to know your stuff when you present to others.

The Five Whys

Working under deadline pressure, it often feels as if we don't have enough time to dive deep and really understand a problem, technology, or situation. There is a balance between knowledge exploration and exploitation; it takes experience to learn when it's necessary to dive deep and when it's better to leave things at an abstract/aggregate level. The Five Whys is an iterative question-asking technique we used at Amazon.com to explore the cause-and-effect relationships underlying a particular problem. It is so called because experience suggests that five is the number of iterations typically required to identify and fix the true root causes of a problem. Here's how it works:

- Write a description of the problem. This helps you formalize the problem and helps ensure that the entire team understands and is focused on the same problem.
- Ask Why the problem happens, and write the answer down below the problem description.
- If the answer you just provided doesn't identify the *root cause* of the problem, ask "why?" again, and write that answer down.
- Loop back through the second and third steps until the team is in agreement that the problem's root cause has been identified. This may take fewer than five Whys or more, depending on the complexity of the problem.

Here's an example of how the Five Whys might work in practice. Suppose you have suffered from a technology outage. The problem description might read, "Customers were unable to access our service for forty-five minutes on Saturday evening." When you ask Why, the first answer might be "There was an unprecedented demand from other services."

However, you and your team might agree that this does not identify the root cause of the service outage. So you ask a second Why, which yields the answer "Our service was dependent upon another service that could not handle the demand."

This in turn forces you to ask a third Why, for which the answer is "The service we were calling did not meet their service SLA."

Which leads to a fourth Why, whose answer is "The other service did not have adequate service capacity to meet their SLA." But so far, this leads us to just put accountability on someone else. *What is* our *accountability?*

And this leads to a fifth Why, which elicits the answer "Because I have not engineered it to handle these conditions and exceptions."

Ah! And there we have it. Finally, after starting with a vague sense of the cause of the problem that basically boils down to a finger-pointing "It was their fault," the real answer finally emerges: "I need to engineer my technology service to gracefully handle any condition that it might be required to address. Now, how do we build that?"

By diving deep into the real conditions and managing the dependencies of others, true answers to problems are found.

Rolling Up the Details

The Amazon annual planning process starts in August and wraps in October. It's an organization-wide deep dive that is designed to create alignment around where resources (including people and capital) are going to be allocated in the coming year. Teams build six-to-eight-page narratives describing their businesses, growth opportunities they envision, their plans for taking advantage of those opportunities, and the resources required.

These narratives work their way up the food chain of leadership culminating in two-pagers that are read at the S-Team level. At each step of the journey, the narratives are examined at strategy meetings, which start with a 15 to 30 minute period of quiet while everyone reads the plan being reviewed. Then discussion begins, which may be far-ranging or focused on one or two features or capabilities out of several. Armed with the detailed written narrative and all the pre-meeting collaboration required to get to this point, the discussions, and ultimately the decisions, are much deeper and more refined than those that emerge from many corporate planning processes.

The enterprise bias for avoiding PowerPoint presentations in favor of written narratives (typically six pages long, sometimes as short as two pages) is a great example of a forcing-function to create an organization that dives deep. As Bezos noted in a 2012 interview with Charlie Rose, "When you have to write your ideas out in complete sentences and complete paragraphs, it forces a deeper clarity of thinking."[2] Narratives force clarity, prioritization, and accountability to deliver, and they force your audience to understand at a deeper level.

Conversely, the dumbing-down of organizations and decision making by overreliance on PowerPoint is well recognized. A retired marine officer voiced his opinions in an essay titled "Dumb-dumb bullets": "PowerPoint is not a neutral tool — it is actively hostile to thoughtful decision-making. It has fundamentally changed our culture by altering the expectations of who makes decisions, what decisions they make and how they make them."[3]

The combination of forcing clarity by using narratives and the roll-up process of planning is how Amazon.com gathers ideas and inputs from throughout the organization, allows innovation to sprout, and brings it all together in order to make the big bets on its future. The moral is clear: at Amazon, no big decision is made without first ensuring that it is based on a deep dive into the underlying details that will determine its success.

"In God We Trust, All Others Must Bring Data"

This well-known management slogan isn't an Amazon leadership principle, but it could be. The ability to combine data, facts, and a customer-centered approach, along with an uncanny ability to dive deep into the details—these are the fundamental tools of leadership at Amazon.com.

13. Have Backbone—
Disagree and Commit

Leaders at Amazon have conviction. They are obligated to respectfully challenge decisions when they disagree, even when doing so is uncomfortable or exhausting; they do not compromise for the sake of social cohesion. But once a decision is made, they commit to it wholeheartedly.

Jeff Bezos likes to describe the Amazon.com culture as friendly and intense, but adds, "If push comes to shove, we'll settle for intense."[1] If you're a member of his S-Team, he expects you to challenge him. He demands a robust conversation.

This is not common in corporate America. In most organizations, senior executives are too terrified to practice dissent in the C-suite. As a consultant, I can't tell you how many CEOs have complained that "no one ever challenges me."

By contrast, Amazon.com is a gladiator culture. No one leaves the coliseum unbloodied, but if you fight hard, you may obtain glory—and at the worst, live to fight another day. But if you refuse to do battle for the emperor altogether, you're guaranteed to be carried out on your shield.

At Amazon.com, I learned that disagreeing with Jeff and the other senior executives was not only beneficial to me personally (as an "owner") but also my obligation to the customer, to the shareholder, and company. "If I drive us over a cliff," Jeff would say, "You're as much at fault as I am."

During my years at Amazon.com, I probably won or witnessed as many gladiatorial combats won with Jeff as lost. More important, my willingness to engage him helped encourage others to do the same. People who watched us interact took heart and began to have the same kinds of robust conversation with him and with others—cautiously at first, more naturally later. That's how you create a healthy top-to-bottom culture—by demonstrating the principles, not just posting them on a wall.

The Importance of Mental Toughness

The backbone necessary to disagree with some of the smartest business minds in the world and commit to your own vision requires an immense amount of mental toughness. Psychotherapist Amy Morin compiled a list of traits that characterize mentally strong people. When I read it, I immediately thought of Amazon.com's gladiator culture. If you want to succeed in Jeff's relentless and fiercely competitive world, you cannot:

- Feel sorry for yourself
- Give away your power
- Shy away from change
- Waste energy on things you cannot control
- Worry about pleasing others
- Fear taking calculated risks
- Dwell on the past
- Make the same mistakes over and over

- Resent others' success
- Give up after failure
- Feel the world owes you anything; or
- Expect immediate results[2]

In a similar vein, psychologist and author Angela Duckworth has done some remarkable research on the importance of what she calls "grit." She argues that success is only partially defined by talent—one's ability to naturally play the piano, hit a curve ball or catch a 20-foot wave. The real test of someone's ability to rise to the top rests more in perseverance—the tenacity they display when confronted by obstacles or conflict.[1] While Duckworth's research focused on the success rates of West Point graduates and spelling bee contestants, I believe her theories would be proven true at Amazon.com as well. The most successful are those who can excel in the pressure cooker, week in and week out, shaking off the occasional failure and the subsequent tongue-lashing, put their heads down, and keep on driving.

14. Deliver Results

Leaders at Amazon focus on the key outputs for their business and deliver them with the right quality and in a timely fashion. Despite setbacks, they rise to the occasion and never settle.

I've told a lot of stories and quoted a lot of Jeff Bezos sayings in an effort to explain what drives the man and the company he has built. But here, at last, is the true heart of the book.

At the end of the day, it's all about outcomes at Amazon. com. If you violate all of the other principles—if you fail to obsess over the customer, communicate vaguely, hire second-rate people, ignore details, and so on—but consistently deliver outstanding business results, then all will be forgiven. After all, the purpose of all the other principles is simply to support and facilitate this final, crucial principle—delivering results.

So my final advice to you is to forget the first 13 principles entirely. "Deliver results" is the only one that *really* matters.

Just kidding.

Sort of.

Conclusion

As you may have figured out, the leadership principles presented here are not secrets—they are publicly posted at Amazon.com and discussed within the company often. The key to these principles lies in the combination of principles and the way they are actually used in making everyday decisions at Amazon. Let me repeat that: *these principles are referred to every day, in real decision-making scenarios, in every corner and at every level of Amazon.*

Like any effective dogma, the leadership principles should be used as a guide, not a blueprint. Even the most enlightened doctrines are going to crash and burn when fundamentalists get their hands on them. Ultimately, Jeff gets this. He probably put it best when said, "If you're not stubborn, you'll give up on experiments too soon. And if you're not flexible, you'll pound your head against the wall and you won't see a different solution to a problem you're trying to solve." Jeff understands that striking a common sense balance is crucial—not trying to follow a set of rules as if they constitute a recipe for success.

Lending too much importance to any one of the principles can up-end the entire framework and ruin the desired effect. For example, if you are *too* vocally self-critical (principle 10), you might endlessly question yourself and sacrifice a bias for action (principle 8). Attempt to earn the trust of others by accepting every task (principle 11), and your high standards could slip (principle 6). You get the picture.

When I was at Amazon in the early to mid-2000s, the leadership principles were used and discussed, but there was no training on them and I don't remember a formal, written list being presented. Today, the principles are referenced and actively used in orientation, training, performance reviews, and so on. A client of mine who ran major technology operations at another high-tech company did a year-long stint at Amazon, and then decided to return to his former employer. Reflecting on his lessons learned over a beer, he told me, "At my current company, I can't even tell you what the company leadership principles are. They were likely developed by a consultant. They certainly aren't used to actively make decisions. What is so unique about Amazon's leadership principles is that they are tactical in nature—they are used every day to make better decisions."

With that, I leave you with one final Jeff-ism on developing your own company culture: "Part of company culture is path-dependent—it's the lessons you learn along the way."[1] These fourteen leadership secrets are some of the lessons that Jeff Bezos and Amazon have learned along the way. I hope you'll find them useful as you make your own journey through today's challenging, dynamic, complex, and incredibly promising business world. May you enjoy some measure of the success that Amazon.com has experienced—and may you have a lot of fun along the way.

Appendix A: Future Ready Self-Service

Author's Note: I originally wrote this document as a white paper at Alvarez and Marsal. I've included it as it is a synthesis of many lessons learned from Amazon. The case example illustrates how we needed to "Think Big" when building the third-party seller platform. Today over 2 million third-party sellers use the tools we created, and their sales represent over 40% of all the product units shipped by Amazon.com.

＊＊

Look closely at Google's purchase of Frommer's and Zagat: It is a window into how customer expectations will continue to evolve over the next eight years.

How? Daisy-chain Google's services together, feed them decades of additional insights enabled by acquisitions like Frommer's and Zagat, and something exponentially more powerful emerges: a completely integrated, "end-to-end-and-back" experience.

A Snapshot of Future-State Customer Service

Picture this: A traveler arrives in Rome, hungry for an authentic Italian meal. A quick search on her smart phone automatically presents restaurant choices in order of their distance from her hotel. Restaurant reviews are also displayed, with those of a few friends and even a fellow traveler she met the day before listed at the top. She taps her choice and discovers the film she saw last week was shot nearby. She finds the eatery with a map app and scopes out the inside and surrounding area using street view. Google Offers notifies her that her favorite Italian dish is the daily special. After her meal, she pays the check using a banking app and is automatically offered the chance to recommend the restaurant to others through various social media apps.

True, much of this picture is familiar today. But in this scenario, every step to her objective—an authentic and memorable experience—is completely contained in the smart phone universe.

Moreover, she is empowered to make free and relevant choices with ease in a foreign country. And she is completely self-sufficient, able to accomplish each of the outcomes most important to her in the exact moment and place she values them most.

Enabling it all? A self-service architecture that understands and serves her well.

The Service-Agile Organization

Welcome to the future of service, where leading companies will be differentiated by the level of immediacy, empowerment, personalization and customization their self-service capabilities offer customers. These "service-agile" companies will also:

- Anticipate and change around customers' needs with unprecedented speed;
- Know which customer interactions are the most valuable and which are most expensive;
- Have a structure and culture promoting the reduction or elimination of manually intensive processes; and
- Provide their customer service agents or customers with easy access to all the information they need to complete a task.

Summary

Here, we explore the impact of self-service on customer experience, operational effectiveness, innovation and agility.

We also examine the fundamental principles of architecting customer-centric services—the scaffolding that impacts customer experience and operational efficiency today, and enables the customer intimacy of the future.

An outline of 10 steps essential to making self-service ready for the near future of customer service follows, along with a brief case study of Amazon.com's creation of a successful self-service architecture for third-party sellers.

Why Self-Service Matters More Than We Thought

Effective self-service does not suffer from a lack of benefits. Lower operating costs alone can be enough to lure any company into developing a self-service architecture. And, as capabilities have evolved, self-service has also improved quality, reduced cycle times and improved customer satisfaction.

Customers Prefer to Serve Themselves

Perhaps most counter-intuitive is the level of customer satisfaction self-service has wrought. Instead of deeming unattended service cold and impersonal, customers have grown accustomed to greater control. In fact, depending on the segment, it appears they prefer it:

- In a recent consumer survey, 2 out of 3 said they prefer self-service over speaking to a person for customer service inquiries.[1]
- 60 percent of consumers surveyed by Corporate Executive Board choose a company's Web self-service as the first method for resolving an issue.[2] A similar survey by Forrester returned 72 percent.[3]

As increasingly advanced mobile devices find their way into more hands around the world, customers will come to expect even greater control over their service experience. Should one company not meet their expectations, a competitor who will can be found with a tap of the finger.

Self-Service Can Define an Organization's Capacity for Growth

Exposing self-service capabilities also drives considerable benefits to the organization as some of these capabilities are already required for internal functions and systems. In mandating customers, agents, and vendors to "do for themselves," companies cannot help but:

- Eliminate non-value-added activities;
- Architect for "exposing" capability and integrating functions and systems automate processes "end-to-end;"
- Create companywide awareness that capabilities must be turned "inside-out" to serve others;
- Eliminate cycle times, reduce errors and eliminate waste;
- Galvanize innovation in measureable and practical ways.

"I am emphasizing the self-service nature of these platforms because it is important for a reason I think is somewhat non-obvious," wrote Jeff Bezos in his 2011 Letter to Shareholders. "Even well-meaning gatekeepers slow innovation. When a platform is self-service, even the improbable ideas can get tried, because there's no expert gatekeeper ready to say, 'That will never work!' Guess what? Many of those improbable ideas do work."[4]

The "side" benefits companies collect on their self-service journey invariably make their organizations more efficient, responsive and innovative in the long run.

Why the Definition of Self-Service Must Change

Customers are not looking for "service." They simply want to get something done or resolve an issue. (Track a package. Change a flight. Fix a problem.) And, they increasingly want to do so quickly and efficiently online so they do not have to make a phone call, send an e-mail or schedule an appointment.

What Passes for Self-Service

Now, consider a more complex interaction. A customer applies for a loan through her bank's website. Once she submits her application, it typically lands on a bank employee's desk and proceeds through several reviews, some automated, some manual – all taking time and incurring cost. The customer must then wait for a call to verify her information and evaluate the parameters of the loan. Then, she waits while her application is reviewed, followed by signatures faxed back and forth…Since the customer was able to begin this process online, many companies would define this as "self-service."

Self-Service Must Flow

But if the loan process above was truly "self-service," the customer would be able to go from the application process to receiving the money, at her own pace, without having to talk to somebody. It would flow from end-to-end.

Layering a self-service capability over one or two steps, without thinking through and integrating the entire process, ultimately requires customers to switch to manual intervention. This does not flow, is not self-service and is all too common:

- Corporate Executive Board reported 57 percent of inbound calls come from customers who first attempt to resolve their issue on a company's website.[5]
- A recent study by The Customer Respect Group found online self-service offered by the majority of auto insurance providers—including State

Farm, Travelers and Nationwide—to actually be unhelpful.[6]

- Forrester indicates that 49 percent of consumers are dissatisfied with help pages and FAQs found on company websites.[7]

What Is Your Self-Service Communicating?

Customers want to accomplish their goals as they define them and as they see fit. Self-service should enable that. When it does not—when the flow is interrupted—the company must ask if it is still in touch with their customers' objectives. And, typically, the customer objective is most vulnerable to compromise in the implementation of self-service. Specifically, due to two common failures:

- *Lack of change leadership.* Despite mounting data to the contrary, the concern that self-service will reduce the amount of service customers receive persists. This alone can create significant roadblocks. So, too, can concerns over a loss of control or the ability to customize. Pushing teams past these misconceptions and fears requires real leadership, and too many implementations falter due to a lack of it.

- *Unwillingness to tackle legacy issues.* From a technical and data standpoint, successfully implementing self-service comes with no lack of challenges. Chief among them is resolving the legacy issues self-service development tends to expose. The tough decisions needed to move forward are too often unexplored.

10 Essential Best Practices of Future-Ready Self-Service

Understanding the customer's objective is vital, and it can be more difficult than many companies realize. Yet, by comparison, it is far simpler than retaining that objective amidst the misconceptions, divergent agendas and difficult decisions involved in self-service implementation. This is where most companies fail and their customers' experiences suffer. According to a recent study[8] by Forrester, that experience can have a profound impact on performance:

- Organizations with the lowest customer experience index scores average a negative annual return of 46 percent, while those at the top averaged an annual return 23 percent higher.
- When firms move from below- to above-average scores, they generate incremental revenue based on customer loyalty ranging from $31M for retailers to $1.4B for hotels.

The role of self-service—the kind that flows all the way to the customer's objective—in customer experience will only continue to grow larger. Enabling "end-to-end" self-service is not easy, but your customers will not accept anything less.

After all, if their experience communicates a lack of understanding of their goals, is it unreasonable for them to wonder if you understand them at all?

Experience creating self-service architecture in multiple environments has revealed 10 best practices essential to an end result that truly serves customer objectives. Some are strategic in nature, while others are more technical and operational. They have been divided accordingly.

1. *Design everything from the customer's perspective.* Involve your customers / partners/vendors in the design of self-service capabilities. Observe them as they try to accomplish activities important to them. Understand their requirements, true goals and get their ideas on how to improve. Then, design services and workflows from the customer's perspective regardless of how systems are owned internally. Expose them only to what will help them reach their objectives (capabilities and choices). Remove everything else.

2. *Rethink policies and the need for manual intervention.* Manage service matters by exception. This will allow the vast majority of customers to make real-time decisions and complete their objectives while you identify the hands-on problems. With the right analytics and algorithms, an automated system can make the repeatable decisions in tandem with a separate exception process for the minority that requires intervention and review.

3. *Require the entire process to be automated.* When the entire process—not just the steps—must be automated, your thinking about what is truly value-added activity will be stretched. Processes that end in non-automated corners become evident and are more easily corrected, resulting in significant improvements in cost and speed. It will force root-cause error reduction and vastly

improve quality. Automating end-to-end is an amazing forcing function for innovation.

4. *Provide a stateless workflow for real-time customer feedback.* Design self-service workflows to support all registration, provisioning, configuration and de-registering processes from the beginning. Then design the underlying services supporting the workflows to manage all states. Also provide customers complete visibility into where they are in the process and how far they are from their objective. Allow them to stop at any point along the way and restart from their last stopping point.

5. *Create a balanced set of metrics for the customer self-service experience.* Create metrics to measure the financial, operational, cost and quality facets of the customer's self-service experience. Break and cascade metrics into detailed sub-processes assigned to specific internal owners. Use routine meetings to review the metrics and encourage peers to challenge each other to improve performance that hurts any phase of the process.

6. *Create and support a program to systematically reduce contacts.* Using methods such as Six Sigma, find and resolve problem areas creating the most contacts by number and cost. Then, design customer interactions so simple, obvious and foolproof that no help documentation is required. In

other words, make the experience "as simple as buying from Amazon.com." Implement "voice-of-the-customer" processes to let customers give direct feedback. This gives response teams empowerment to direct change and prioritization efforts across the company. Proper organizational support for this group is critical, since they are addressing the verifiable pain endured by customers.

7. *Unlock data and systems through Service-Oriented Architectures (SOA) and Web Services.* Externalizing processes managed by legacy systems is one of the biggest technical challenges in self-service, but it can be done. Invest in wrapping legacy systems using an SOA approach, so that developers can more readily access the underlying data and business logic. SOA architecture will also simplify the customer experience by abstracting and hiding the underlying complexity.

8. *Invest in user interface design to make all interactions outstanding.* Insist on user experience excellence in all interactions, including vendors, partners and employees. This increases the number who use self-service, requiring far less support from your organization. Requiring this level of consistency develops the habits and culture of "design excellence." Steve Jobs demanded the inside of the computer be as simple and beautiful as the outside. Why? It created a company-wide

culture of design excellence and attention to detail.

9. *Analyze data to create new customer insights.* Collect as much data about customer self-service interaction as possible. Use this data to understand how the customer interacts with the system one way or another. Use this information to provide the feedback to both the customer and internal teams. Show the customer this data in a transparent way, including benchmark information, and set a high bar for the performance and reliability of the self-service platform. Consistently measure and review the "to-the-glass" performance of your services. Relentlessly focus on raising the bar by measuring and reporting against the worst, not the best, customer experience.

10. *Integrated and agile solution development.* Break the long cycle, big-bang project waterfall mentality by investing in agile development methods. Create integrated project teams between business, technology and operations. Make these truly integrated and break the traditional fences and rules of engagement. Challenge the organization to deliver significant benefit in no more than three-month segments. Engage tough problem sets early and seek speed to market. A bias for action will allow you to "see around the corner" and uncover problems others have not confronted yet, which in turn drives innovation.

CASE STUDY—AMAZON.COM: A PROFILE IN SELF-SERVICE ARCHITECTURE FOR THIRD-PARTY SELLERS

The Problem

In early 2002, Amazon.com wanted to open its online marketplace up to thousands of third-party merchants. The new, self-service, "Selling on Amazon" program had to meet a rigorous design objective:

A new seller had to be able to register, list and sell products in the middle of the night, with no one at Amazon knowing or assisting.

In other words, each step—from start to final sale—had to be 100 percent self-service.

This was a huge program impacting vast systems at Amazon, including website, item management, payment, customer service, fraud and ordering systems. The registration workflow alone required automation and integration of approximately 40 different backend systems. To add to that, new Amazon.com sellers possessed various levels of technical ability.

The Solution

The team decided to build different paths and tools for a range of seller types.

This required a complex set of requirements, a deep understanding of both the customer experience and seller experience, and a healthy dose of ambition.

By designing for self-service from the beginning, the team created clear and easily understood automations—well beyond what an internal-only process would have required. Key self-service capabilities built included:

- Registration: A state-full workflow for a seller to register and begin listing, selling, and getting paid by Amazon.
- Documentation: A robust set of documentation and application programming interface (API) guides, including reference implementation material.
- Test environments and validation: Documented test cases, feedback and many test harnesses and tools to help sellers practice on the system before they started selling to real customers.
- Different integration methods: API driven, file upload or "1 x 1 graphical user interface (GUI)" tools sellers could either use or automate.
- Feedback and account management: A "Seller Central" portal environment in which a seller could manage his relationship with Amazon, including key settings, reports and notifications.
- Extensive real-time data: Providing orders, customer feedback and other operational information to help sellers do better and make more money.

The Results

In 18 months, Amazon.com went from not having any third-party sellers to having tens of thousands in more than 12 different categories.

"This was in 2002, 2003 and 2004, when I had the opportunity to play a key role in launching and scaling that side of the business," said John Rossman, Managing Director at Alvarez & Marsal and former Director of Merchant Integration at Amazon.com. "Today, it accounts for 40 percent of all Amazon.com units sold." Within five years, that share of overall sales is expected to grow to 55 percent.[9]

Takeaways

Self-service is no longer a "nice-to-have." Customers not only accept self-service, they expect it. As access to more advanced, web-savvy mobile devices increases, the demand for control over the kind of interaction they choose and the time it takes to reach their objective will only continue to grow.

Self-service must be "end-to-end." Yet what too many companies accept as self-service will simply not be sufficient to keep pace with the rise and change of their customers' expectations.

Rather than a piecemeal approach layering self-service capability over one or two areas of the process, "service-agile" companies integrate self-service processes from end-to-end. They will enable their customers to not only begin a process, but also reach their ultimate objective without ever being required to "talk" to someone.

The 10 essential best practices of future-ready self-service

In our experience of creating self-service architectures in multiple environments, we have identified 10 best practices—strategic and technical—essential to leading a service-agile organization:

1. Design everything from the customer perspective
2. Rethink policies and the need for manual intervention
3. Require the entire process to be automated
4. Provide a stateless workflow providing real-time customer feedback
5. Create a balanced set of metrics for the customer self-service experience
6. Create and support a program to systematically reduce contacts
7. Unlock data and systems through Service-Oriented Architectures (SOA) and Web Services
8. Invest in user interface design to make all interactions outstanding
9. Create great usage metrics
10. Integrated and agile solution development

Conclusion

Enabling the capabilities essential to end-to-end self-service is not easy. It requires change at a level many companies have yet to consider.

Meanwhile, companies that have made the change are already reaping the benefits of increased revenue, lower costs to serve and greater market share. And they have, in turn, become more efficient, performance-oriented and customer-focused.

As customer expectations continue to rise, self-service is no longer a "nice-to-have." Rather, end-to-end self-service capabilities will only play an increasingly central role in who retains more customers, fosters innovation and spurs growth.

Appendix B: Free Cash Flow

A uthor's Note: I wrote this document with my colleagues at Alvarez and Marsal, Ryan Scott and Randy Miller. It offers a more detailed discussion of free cash flow (FCF) including more background and examples, than I had room to provide when introducing the topic in chapter 7.

◂▴▸

Mass retail is a notoriously low margin, efficiency based business. Keeping large margins over a long period of time is difficult, and likely results in a smaller market share. From the beginning, Amazon has set a course and vision to be "the biggest store in the world", starting as a book store and now including all categories. Tied to this philosophy is a perspective about optimizing financial results. Jeff Bezos sums up the strategy this way:

"Percentage margins are not one of the things we are seeking to optimize. It's the absolute dollar free cash flow per share that you want to maximize. If you can do that by lowering margins, we would do that. Free cash flow, that's something investors can spend."[1]

Free Cash Flow Defined

Free Cash Flow (FCF) can be calculated in a few ways, with most calculation methods designed for investors who are looking to untangle the accounting tricks used to generate Financial Statements. For the business manager, we will focus on the following definition:

$$FCF = (Revenue - Cost - Depr.) * (1 - \tau_c) + Depr. - CapEx - \Delta NWC \quad \text{[Eqn. 1]}$$

where: τ_c = tax rate
Depr. = depreciation
NWC = Net Working Capital

[Note that depreciation is added back in because it is a non-cash expenditure. It is for this reason that FCF is not the same as other measures commonly used by investors to evaluate the health and success of a business such as EBITDA, Net Earnings, and Profit Margin Percentage.

Rearranging terms in Eqn. 1, we arrive at a basic definition of Free Cash Flow:

$$FCF = \underbrace{(Revenue - Cost) * (1 - \tau_c)}_{\text{Cash from Operations}} - \underbrace{CapEx - \Delta NWC}_{\text{Operating Expenditures}} + \underbrace{\tau_c * Depr.}_{\text{Tax Shield}} \quad \text{[Eqn. 2]}$$

'Revenue - Cost' represents cash generated from operations, CapEx and ΔNWC is the money spent to keep the business running, and the final term in Eqn. 2 is the cash contribution that 'depreciation as a tax shield' represents.

A business's day-to-day operations, such as the sale of products and sale of services, are the source of FCF and Operating Expenditure is cash spent to run and maintain the business on a day-to-day basis. FCF, however, is the remaining cash available, and is free to be spent in ways that add value for the business. Stated simply, FCF is free to be spent in ways that grow real value for shareholders.

In his 2004 Letter to Shareholders, Bezos explains the reason for Amazon's focus on FCF: "Why not focus first and foremost, as many do, on earnings, earnings per share or earnings growth? The simple answer is that earnings don't directly translate into cash flows, and shares are worth only the present value of their future cash flows, not the present value of their future earnings."

"Our ultimate financial measure, and the one we most want to drive over the long-term, is free cash flow per share.

Free Cash Flow as Amazon's Business Engine

Free Cash Flow can be a powerful engine for driving shareholder value. At Amazon, it is both the proverbial North Star that managers use to guide operations, and the fuel that leadership uses to drive business strategy.

The following figure shows how FCF moves from Operations to Business Strategy which in turn grows and improves Operations.

Operations Generate Free Cash Flow. Now that we've established that Operations is the source of Free Cash Flow, the next step is to set up appropriate measurements and KPIs. A few examples from Amazon include contribution profit and total sales rather than contribution margin as a percentage.

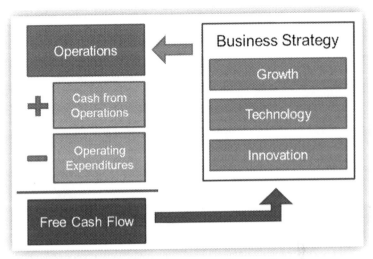

Figure B-1. Free Cash Flow as a Business Engine

This focus on FCF as the primary financial measure at Amazon began in earnest when Warren Jenson became CFO in October of 1999. As noted above in the Bezos' quote, it is also the time when the Amazon finance organization began to move away from a "percentage" margin focus to a "cash" margin focus. Bezos loved to toss out the axiom "percentages don't pay the light bill, cash does!" He would then ask "Do you want to be a $200 million company with a 20% margin or a $10 billion company with a 5% margin? I know which one I want to be!"

This new direction of putting FCF at the center of Amazon's strategy, as well as the need to manage it successfully, drove the creation of powerful measurement and modeling capabilities. One powerful example of this is the robust and extremely accurate 'unit economic' model that was developed. This tool allows merchants, finance analysts, and optimization modelers to understand how different buying decisions, process flows, fulfillment paths, and demand scenarios will affect a product's contribution profit. This in turn gave Amazon the ability to understand how changes in these variables would impact FCF, and has allowed them to react accordingly.

Very few retailers have this type of in-depth financial view of their products, and thus have a difficult job truly making decisions or building processes that optimize the economics. Amazon uses this knowledge to determine the number of warehouses and where they should be placed, to quickly assess and respond to vendor offers, to develop a better understanding of inventory margin health, to know how much it will cost them to hold a unit of inventory over a specified period of time down to the penny, and so forth and so on.

Free Cash Flow as the Fuel for Business Strategy. Let us now assume that Operations are running efficiently and FCF is being generated. As a leader, it is your responsibility to spend this cash in whatever way creates the most value for shareholders. Your options fall into 4 basic categories:

- Investing in growth
- Paying down debt
- Buying back shares
- Paying out dividends

Investing in growth is the most interesting option here, and has been the core of Amazon's business strategy to date. Bezos believes that a company will stagnate without constant innovation, and that the primary ingredient for strong innovation is free cash flow. Many would argue that spending FCF on buying back shares or paying out dividends is a signal that senior leadership has run out of positive NPV projects, and that shareholders are better off finding better uses for their money.

At Amazon, common areas of investment have included adding new categories, new businesses, new infrastructure (such as fulfillment centers), and scale through technology. New businesses are incubated for a period of time in order to prove their viability and optimize operations before FCF is invested to scale to a national or global level. Amazon Fresh is a perfect example of this, having been run locally in Seattle since 2007 before expanding to other cities in 2013.

Free Cash Flow as a Decision Driver

As a business leader, one of your main responsibilities is to make sound and reasonable decisions for the management of your company. It's a given that these decisions should be based on data, goals, and KPI's, and competitive insights—but which ones? Let's take an in-depth look at how a C-level decision can vary with the following two goals:

- Maximize Net Earnings
- Maximize Free Cash Flow

To compare these alternative decision drivers, let us analyze a hypothetical business scenario from Jeff Bezos's 2004 Letter to Amazon Shareholders:

> Imagine that an entrepreneur invents a machine that can quickly transport people from one location to another. The machine is expensive—$160 million with an annual capacity of 100,000 passenger trips and a four year useful life. Each trip sells for $1,000 and requires $450 in cost of goods for energy and materials and $50 in labor and other costs.

Continue to imagine that business is booming, with 100,000 trips in Year 1, completely and perfectly utilizing the capacity of one machine. This leads to earnings of $10 million after deducting operating expenses including depreciation—a 10% net margin.

Although overly simplified, this business scenario allows us to take a closer look at the decision process.

Maximize Net Earnings. It is now the end of Year 1 and the entrepreneur must make a decision. If the company's primary goal is to maximize earnings, then the best course of action is to invest more capital to add additional machines, fuel sales, and grow earnings. Let us assume that the entrepreneur decides to grow the business by 100% each year, purchasing an additional machine in Year 2, two more in Year 3, and four more in Year 4.

Here is the income statement for the first four years of business when earnings growth is the company goal:

	Earnings			
	Year 1	Year 2	Year 3	Year 4
	(in thousands)			
Sales	$100,000	$200,000	$400,000	$800,000
Units sold	100	200	400	800
Growth	N/A	100%	100%	100%
Gross profit	55,000	110,000	220,000	440,000
Gross margin	55%	55%	55%	55%
Depreciation	40,000	80,000	160,000	320,000
Labor & other costs	5,000	10,000	20,000	40,000
Earnings	$ 10,000	$ 20,000	$ 40,000	$ 80,000
Margin	10%	10%	10%	10%
Growth	N/A	100%	100%	100%

Table B-1. 2004 Letter to Shareholders

If this transport machine is truly revolutionary, it is reasonable to assume that demand can keep up with capacity. In the first 4 years of operation, the company sees 100% compound earnings growth and $150 million of cumulative earnings! It appears that the sky is the limit for this company. Let's see what things look like when maximizing FCF is the goal.

Maximizing Free Cash Flow. To analyze this business through the Free Cash Flow lens, let's take a look at the Cash Flow statement for Years 1 through 4 with the additional machine purchases included:

	Cash Flows			
	Year 1	Year 2	Year 3	Year 4
		(in thousands)		
Earnings	$ 10,000	$ 20,000	$ 40,000	$ 80,000
Depreciation	40,000	80,000	160,000	320,000
Working capital	—	—	—	—
Operating Cash Flow	50,000	100,000	200,000	400,000
Capital expenditures	160,000	160,000	320,000	640,000
Free Cash Flow	$(110,000)	$ (60,000)	$(120,000)	$(240,000)

Table B-2. 2004 Letter to Shareholders

Free Cash Flow tells a very different story from the one told by Earnings. FCF is negative in Year 1 because of the massive capital expenditure in the transport machine. The machine is already being run at full capacity, and only has an operating life of 4 years so even with 0% growth, the net present value of cash flows (assuming 12% cost of capital) is still negative.

To improve FCF, we can focus on improving Cash from Operations, or on reducing Operating Expenditures. Probing in these two areas leads to questions such as:

- How much would the production cost of the transportation machine need to be reduced by for this to be a positive FCF business?
- How much should the price of a ticket be raised to for this to be a positive FCF business? What is the price elasticity of near instant transportation?
- Would the transportation machine last longer if it wasn't run at full capacity? What if it turned out that running at 80% capacity doubled the operating life of the machine? How would this effect FCF?

With maximizing FCF as the goal, our manager would have made very different investment decisions then when maximizing Earnings was the goal. Without other options or modifications to this business model, we see that, in this scenario, committing capital to growth is a poor choice. Rather than investing in growth, the best course is to invest in improving and optimizing the business model to see if this business model can become FCF positive.

Appendix C. The Critical Capabilities of Building and Operating a Platform Company

The development of the "capabilities-as-a-business" market is rapidly accelerating the rate of innovation in business. Whether it is "cloud computing" as a service, or more process-oriented capabilities such as "delivery as a service" or "content management as a service," leaders are driving change and competing faster, cheaper, and with lower risk by utilizing "platforms."

As I detailed in multiple chapters of the book, Amazon.com and Jeff Bezos have famously catalyzed strategy and execution of a "platform." Additionally, we developed these platform strategies and capabilities during my tenure running the third-party selling business and then the enterprise services business—where we managed other large retailers' ecommerce infrastructures (Target.com, Toys R Us.com, Marks & Spencer).

However, Amazon.com is actually several different platforms. There is the "retail platform business" which allows the roughly 2 million third-party sellers to leverage the customer base and infrastructure of Amazon.com to sell products, plus

Amazon the retailer to sell and deliver. There is also the "merchant services" platform which brings both holistic and component capabilities to ecommerce capabilities that clients use to build and run their ecommerce business. Example capabilities include "checkout by Amazon," "fulfillment by Amazon," and "payments by Amazon." There is the cloud computing infrastructure business at Amazon known as AWS (Amazon Web Services), a computing and technology infrastructure that is the market leader in cloud capabilities. Example AWS capabilities include "compute," "storage," and sophisticated managed services such as the "big data infrastructure" known as Elastic Map Reduce and Redshift, that allow a company to rapidly provision infrastructure that is well beyond the engineering capability of most companies to bring together.

Yet creating a platform is a far more comprehensive change than simply adding a technology or altering operations. It transforms your sales model and the channels you utilize; it alters your project management and changes the very nature of your relationships and revenue. It also requires patience and a long-term strategy. It changes *everything*.

To fully understand the catalyzing force of the platform, it is important to define its key differences and critical capabilities. In today's world of hype-driven, buzzword marketing, it seems as if everyone is calling their business a "platform." *Yet what are the critical differences between a platform company and a normal technology and data services company?*

The framework and outline below seek to answer this question. However, I doubt that any company embodies 100 percent of these factors. In fact, it may not be beneficial to embody all of these factors. Moreover, "being a platform" may not be the right strategy for your company at all. That said, this framework will help you evaluate *if* and *how* to either transition to being a platform company, or work with a platform company.

The segmentation of these capabilities fall into the groups shown in Figure C-1:

Business Model	Attributes of the business model that differentiate a pltform business.
Operational	Attributes of "operating the company" that differentiate a platform business.
Ecosystem	Attributes of the ecosystem highly impacted or differentiates platform business.
Critical Capabilities	Capabilities or features important to end customers or ecosystem partners.

Figure C-1. Platform capabilities segmentation.

Changes to the Business Model

A wide variety of businesses are looking for ways to re-invent using a platform model. While launching a platform business requires new cost structures and revenue models, it also requires patience and a fresh perspective. The following attributes differentiate a platform business from a more traditional technology business model.

Fixed Cost. A platform business is characterized by having a largely fixed cost business, with little or no marginal costs for each additional user of the platform. While there is significant capital and R&D in building the platform, the business then operates on the "network effect." A platform's popularity and effectiveness increases exponentially in relation to the number of tenants it supports. Consider Facebook. The more users, the better the experience, the larger the network grows—it's more or less a self-perpetuating system. Once the platform is established, costs are marginal. In other words, much of your investment is up front.

Depending upon the business, these initial fixed costs may be in manufacturing infrastructure (TSMC, Samsung, Intel), distribution network and fleet assets (i.e. FedEx, UPS), telecommunications (ATT, Verizon, Cox), content (i.e. NetFlix, Hulu), and certainly technology infrastructures (Amazon, Amazon Web Services). Out of this list, only Amazon has organized itself as a platform company.

Marginal Costs. While marginal costs for each customer do exist, these per customer marginal costs decrease over time as the scale of adoption and scale of the platform increases. This is often accomplished by simple, leveraged purchasing and vendor management, but can also occur by incorporating increasing commodity elements into the infrastructure and building the IP in the proprietary platform management layers. Continuously reducing the IP of third-party components, and building these capabilities into your platform capability, is a classic move of driving toward commoditization and reducing dependencies on other partners.

For example, Amazon Web Services decreases marginal costs of additional technology infrastructure by continuing to use highly scalable commoditized infrastructure and by building the proprietary cloud fabric managing the infrastructure. In the case of Microsoft, marginal costs include the development of new software or even producing the jewel cases to package their disks.

Hidden Platform. The end customer is often unaware of the underlying platform being used. An indicator of a platform business is that end customers and clients are (or can be) significantly ignorant of the underlying platform provider. This creates a marketing challenge perhaps best exemplified by the "Intel Inside" campaign or the fact that Netflix uses Amazon Web Services as a platform—a fact that few if any customers realize. Direct marketing, traditional sales may not be as necessary as traditional marketing and sales channels. Building the interactions with the platform as "self-service" as possible, helps enable flexibility and scaling.

Revenue Model. For a platform business, revenue is collected in a more continuous stream with smaller amounts, rather than the lumpy quarterly collections from new sales that often make up 90 percent of revenue. Revenue tends to be more recurring revenue and subscription based than a 'one-time' license or service revenue found in traditional software or services companies. Because of the network effect mentioned above, "customer satisfaction" is perhaps more important than in traditional non-platform businesses.

Platform businesses must also adjust to the transient nature of customers. Simplicity of provisioning to the platform services lowers barriers to access and use and result in casual or seasonal usage. A successful platform business will see a significant percentage of revenue fluctuate as these casual users migrate and must shift marketing and operating focus to support this new class of customers.

Lastly, platform companies may need to adjust to a lower margin and higher volume mix of business as well as look at capital investments return over a longer horizon than may have been typical.

Long-Term Strategy. Platform businesses often need to take a longer term, phased view regarding capital investment and product development. Delivering scalable and reliable services over time requires careful upfront planning and design with phased long-term execution. The platform must be able to be run economically at both small and large scale.

It also requires significant investment to build a compelling platform. Once you have achieved this, you must allow time for the flywheel to engage. A platform business is not the fast way to revenue. It requires a long-term strategy.

Operational Changes

Establishing a platform business requires different operational attributes or core processes than a traditional business model. When offering a platform service, it is vital to be far more wired to customer and internal metrics while ensuring seamless continuity, high performance and a high degree of availability.

Service Level Agreements (SLAs). Well-defined and granular operational service levels, security and privacy controls, along with key real-time operating data availability is critical to allow others to trust and operate on a platform. If third parties cannot manage and have the operational controls of the environment, the ability to "bet the business" is significantly compromised. Best-in-class platforms offer service levels and operational control exceeding what a typical company can practically build and deliver for itself. This is a key value proposition for using the platform.

Business Continuity. Platform businesses must target 100 percent service availability. This means planning for service failures while being able to seamlessly shift customers to alternative services. Ideally, the customer should not know which services are being used or where they are located. Business continuity becomes about overall service network redundancy and durability. The importance of this aspect of a platform cannot be overstated. Consider the outcry when Facebook is down or the revenue lost if the Amazon.com site crashes for even a few hours.

High Performance and Availability. Platforms offer availability and performance attributes that non-platforms cannot offer (at comparable costs). However, to compete with the latter, successful platforms must work well and always work. New features and system maintenance should be accommodated without adverse impact to customers to maintain business continuity. Exemplary performance is key to the retention of tenants, which tend to be more transient—especially if a competitive platform exists. It is also at the core of any platform's value proposition and constitutes a great deal of its competitive advantage. The gold standard of web service platforms, for example, is Amazon's AWS, which offers a degree of performance and availability that typical companies cannot begin to match.

Instrumentation as a Core Competency. As a core competency, the platform and organization builds and runs the business with world-class monitoring, metrics, analytics and self-monitoring capabilities. These capabilities and data are appropriately exposed to partners and clients. In short, you must measure and monitor everything in order to assess and improve performance. Without proper instrumentation, your platform is "flying blind."

Service Analytics. Transparency is key. Platform customers must have the same level of visibility into platform performance, exception management, and end customer behaviors as the service providers themselves. Some aspects of the service should be a "black box," but platform customers need to be able to implement efficient feedback loops and be able to analyze their interface with the platform to facilitate continuous improvement. Fortunately, the very nature of a platform business allows for comprehensive monitoring—if the instrumentation is in place.

Multi-tenant. Capabilities of a multi-tenant platform include the ability to add a substantial amount of clients, brands, or "eco-system partners" without modification, separate infrastructure or new "instances." A platform facilitates multiple tenants with custom configuration, business rules and functionality—without changing the underlying platform. This often requires the ability to "co-mingle" clients while providing the required "separation" of critical data or proprietary capability. Consequently, this shared infrastructure requires the proper placement of governance, data management or public policies to minimize conflict and disruption on the common infrastructure.

Global Platform. An indicator of a platform business is that a common execution and code base is used, resulting in an entirely consistent interface. This results in a "one instance" model versus multiple deployed instances running parallel to another. This massively scalable technology offering is easy to operate, upgrade and deploy; as important, it requires only "one bug, one fix" solutions. The result is a well-oiled machine that provides seamless interface and user experience—key aspects to business continuity. AWS, for example, could lose a complete data center and the customer would never know it. In fact, Amazon.com occasionally tests that theory by purposely shutting off data centers.

Zero Provisioned. Adding a partner or client has zero provisioning costs for the platform company due to the self-service attribute. In other words, an external entity that wants to use your capabilities should be able to sign up and use them without your assistance (see Appendix A, "Future Ready Self-Service").

"Eat Your Own Dog Food." Be your own customer. Internally, all developers must use APIs to access services and capabilities just as an external developer would. This inherently makes the capabilities better. Using your own platform provides detailed internal feedback and drives ever more robust capabilities. Amazon.com's move into the Web services business (offering storage, payment and bandwidth infrastructure to other companies in what has come to be known as cloud computing), was initially a response to the company's own technology needs.

Core Capabilities as Services. Platform businesses need to approach product management in a different way than traditional product companies. Companies need to define the core, value-adding capabilities that they currently have or could develop, and determine how to expose capabilities as comprehensive and complete services. Thinking broadly about potential services is important.

The Attributes of a Platform Ecosystem

A platform company not only enables, but also facilitates other businesses' use of their platform. Ideally, a strong platform attracts deeply invested third parties that innovate and construct new capabilities on top of it. For example, Amazon Web Services, Fulfillment by Amazon, and Kindle Direct Publishing create powerful self-service platforms that allow large numbers of users to experiment and accomplish things that would otherwise be impossible or impractical. In his 2011 Shareholder Letter, Amazon.com's Jeff Bezos explained how "innovative, large-scale platforms are not zero-sum—they create win-win situations and create significant value for developers, entrepreneurs, customers, authors, and readers." Consequently, one of the keys is to actively identify the types of partners who can build on your platform—those opportunities become your channel expertise.

External Innovation. Not only do other enterprises provide a new channel or "sell" the platform (as in the cases of traditional VAR or channel partners), but actually innovate on the platform as well—without anyone in the platform organization needing to know about it. In other words, there are no gatekeepers. Bezos has consistently emphasized the self-service nature of platforms because "even well-meaning gatekeepers slow innovation." In his 2011 Shareholder Letter, he goes on to explain, "When a platform is self-service, even the improbable ideas can get tried, because there's no expert gatekeeper ready to say, "That will never work!" And guess what—many of those improbable ideas do work, and society is the beneficiary of that diversity."

Natural Synergies. A platform business creates both intentional and unintentional synergies—a virtuous cycle or flywheel. These synergies increase the value and traction of the platform with each additional partner. For example, using "Fulfillment by Amazon" allows a seller's items to be "Prime" eligible at Amazon. Being Prime eligible increases the sale of the item at Amazon.com. Increasing the sales is good for both the seller and for Amazon.com (and the end customer). Again, the more a platform is used, the more its fixed costs are covered, and the more efficiently the flywheel turns. Increased use increases use.

An Open and Level Playing Field. The rules, potential conflicts and competition between the platform, policies, and ecosystem partners should be fair, well governed and slow moving. Ecosystem partners must be able to bet on the platform with low risk of being cannibalized. If you want other companies betting their futures on you, you have to be transparent and fair. As a prime example of getting this wrong, many experts point to Mark Zuckerberg's 2007 launch of Facebook Platform. While the initial idea was promising—effectively allowing any developer to build full applications on top of the social graph, inside the Facebook framework—the execution was undermined within 18 months when the company abandoned the idea of a level playing field and added new features that restricted the capabilities of developers who were building similar products. Today, Facebook Platform is considered a missed opportunity representing tens of billions of dollars of lost revenue.

Unplanned Customers and Innovation. Peter Drucker wrote that the unexpected was the richest source of opportunity for successful innovation. Prepare for customers and innovation you haven't even dreamed of or have yet to exist. Successful platforms should expect to be "surprised" by new and different types of innovation and capabilities. This requires the business to be effective in identifying new customer segments and nimble in responding to new demand channels. Creating both the environment and tools (such as API's) which make it easy for customers and partners to use and innovate without your direct involvement is the new paradigm for management.

Critical Capabilities

There are several important facets that a successful platform is required to offer. These product capabilities promote innovation, growth, data measurement, adoption rates, compliance and security. Without them, any platform will struggle to effectively engage its flywheel.

APIs and Bulk Operations. The clearly defined "sockets" or interfaces through which others interact with the platform are often hardened APIs. APIs are the essential enabler of exposing capability in a useable manner to allow others to leverage it. APIs can expose data, logic, processes and other types of either high-level or low-level capabilities. While having APIs is critical, the right APIs coupled with other key strategic and tactical capabilities are needed to develop a platform business model.

However, APIs are not the only interfaces. Portals, documentation, SLAs, and real-time operational data are all examples of additional aspects of hardened interfaces. "Hardened" means that the interface is durable and evolves over time, but possesses a well-established roadmap and change control. These capabilities are typically backwards compatible, and should always be "obvious" to the user.

Analytics. Platforms need to empower customers and their ecosystem by providing robust and deep analytics—far deeper and real-time than providers are engineered to typically deliver.

Self-Service. A platform business creates scale and operating efficiencies by being "self-service" for partners, clients and users of the platform. Clientele should be able to graduate from "discovery to operating" without ever talking to someone at the platform business. Often, communities are formed to help provide collaboration, but these communities are often independent of the platform company and build excitement and awareness (see Appendix A, "Future Ready Self-Service").

By-The-Sip Pricing. Part of the value proposition of a platform business is that the service transforms what are traditionally fixed capital and operating costs to flexible and variable expensed costs. The ability to quickly scale, both up AND down, is a key aspect of the model. The scaling should be able to happen with a much shorter lead time than is traditionally needed for the capability. This provides greater flexibility to the client by switching traditional fixed "capital" costs to more elastic, "by-the-sip" operating expenses. For example, if a "fulfillment center" capability is the service, a company would traditionally need to build and capitalize distribution centers and equipment, with a typical year to multi-year lead time. "Fulfillment-As-A-Service" allows a client to vary fulfillment capability, dial-up and dial-down fulfillment capacity, and do so with a very short lead time (one month to one day). In addition, platforms do not require clients to sign a huge contract, which promotes use.

Compliance Capability "As a Service." In the heightened legal, global and compliance atmosphere in which we operate, platform businesses provide clients with an unusually high control and assurance for meeting and supporting compliance, as well as audit and tax management. Both governance and compliance are facilitated by the platform's inherent metrics and instrumentation. Similarly, a platform must be able to demonstrate a high degree of data security.

Data and content stewardship. Attracting tenants to a platform requires a high degree of trust in your service offering. It is vital that a platform provides clearly expressed and easily managed policies and assurances on data protection, reconciliation, and delete rights.

Change Enabler. Be a door, not a wall. Whether via acquisition/divestiture or structural change, the platform should be an enabler and not a constraint to structural realignment of the user organization. Data models, configuration, archiving, and key capabilities are designed to accommodate and manage change.

Summary

Becoming a platform company is not just a major change, **it changes everything!** Sales, marketing, product management, operations, roles, responsibilities, measures—all are impacted by shifting one's strategy to being a platform company. Creating capabilities that others leverage "as a service" creates tremendous opportunity in innovation, truly changing the way work gets done.

What are the opportunities in your industry? By looking at the value chain of an industry and seeing where the inefficiencies, brokers and "gatekeepers" are trapping customers, we can develop strategies to continuously innovate with a platform. Take, for example, Amazon apparel. We started the business as just another third-party seller platform. Then Amazon started selling inventory they sourced. Now, they are designing their own proprietary product and building apparel-specific process capabilities such as Amazon Photo Studios that others can easily leverage as a service. It is very difficult to get building platforms right. Companies that might be assumed at being good at this have largely missed. Steve Yegge, a senior Google engineer and former Amazon engineer, articulated how "That one last thing that Google doesn't do well is Platforms. We don't understand platforms. We don't "get" platforms."[1] Facebook pronounced in 2007 that they were going to be an open platform. How many companies are making their business on the Facebook platform?[2]

Make no mistake. We are "Day One" in building and using platform capabilities to fundamentally reinvent how work gets done. *What is your strategy?*

Acknowledgements

I'm an industrial engineer by education and a consultant by profession. I create too many PowerPoint decks for a living, which means that writing in bullet points comes far more naturally to me than writing a book.

This project really started when Clifford Cancelosi, my great friend, a colleague at Amazon and then at Alvarez and Marsal, sat with me in my home office one rainy Seattle day to brainstorm the principles that became the article "Future-Ready Self-Service" (Appendix A in this book). Writing that piece helped me realize how much I'd learned at Amazon, and that I had a story to tell. Clifford contributed many stories and helped me clarify many of the concepts that appear in these pages. Without his ideas and suggestions, the contents of this book would be far less rich and interesting.

Greg Shaw at the Bill & Melinda Gates Foundation and now at Microsoft was one of the first to encourage me to write the book. He saw the leadership principles as the central theme to build around, and he was critical in helping me pull together the team.

Tom Elsenbrook, who runs the business consulting business at Alvarez and Marsal, recognized the potential of the project and helped me navigate making this happen.

Randy Miller, another ex-Amazon colleague and Alvarez and Marsal colleague, was an early finance and category leader at Amazon and has been very generous in sharing his time and experiences.

The talented writer Ryan Masters played the critical role in transforming my raw content and stories into a coherent

Acknowledgements

and interesting book. He understood the messages I was trying to convey, the needs of the audience I was trying to reach, and the kinds of anecdotes and examples that would help bring the key themes vividly to life. Thanks for your essential help, Ryan!

My editor Karl Weber polished the prose and provided fantastic feedback to improve the story.

John Rossman
March, 2014

About the Author

John Rossman works with companies to develop and implement innovative business models, technology strategies, and operations improvement for Fortune 500 companies in industry sectors ranging from high tech, to philanthropy to retail. He currently works as a managing director for Alvarez & Marsal, a global, professional services firm that delivers performance improvement, turnaround management, and business advisory services to organizations seeking to transform operations, catapult growth, and accelerate results through decisive action.

Prior to A&M, John served as director of enterprise services at Amazon.com, where he developed the Merchants @ program, a B2B network that enables millions of sellers to offer products through Amazon, which now is over 40 percent of all orders. He also ran the relationships with enterprise clients like Target.com, Toys "R" Us, Sears.ca, Marks and Spencer, and the NBA.

John lives in Seattle, Washington with his wife and two boys. He holds a BS in industrial engineering from Oregon State University.

Sources

Introduction

[1] "Amazon Leadership Principles," at http://www.amazon.jobs/principles.

Chapter 1

[1] Bill Price and David Jaffe, *The Best Service is No Service: How to Liberate Your Customers from Customer Service, Keep Them Happy, and Control Costs*, Jossey-Bass, March 21, 2008.

[2] "Inside Amazon's Idea Machine," *Forbes*, April 23, 2012.

[3] 1997 Letter to Shareholders, Jeff Bezos, Amazon.com, March 30, 1998.

[4] "Amazon Losing Its Price Edge," *The Wall Street Journal*, August 20, 2013.

[5] http://franklincovey.com/blog/consultants/toddwangsgard/2010/02/12/pulling-andon-cord-lessons-timeout/

[6] http://www.amazon.com/gp/jobs/228529?ie=UTF8&category=Customer%20Service&jobSearchKeywords=&location=US&page=1

[7] 2012 Letter to Shareholders, Jeff Bezos, Amazon.com, April 12, 2012.

[8] "Inside the Mind of Jeff Bezos," *Fast Company*, August 1, 2004.

[9] Ibid.

[10] David LaGesse, "America's Best Leaders: Jeff Bezos, Amazon.com CEO," *U.S. News*, November 19, 2008.

[11] Chuck Salter, "Most Innovative Companies 2009: Amazon #9," *Fast Company*, February 10, 2009.

Chapter 2

[1] Nicholas Carlson, "Jeff Bezos's Salary Is Only $14,000 More Than The Average Facebook Intern's," *Business Insider*, April 15, 2013

[2] Brad Stone, *The Everything Store: Jeff Bezos and the Age of Amazon*, Little, Brown and Company, October 15, 2013.

[3] "Jeff Bezos 'Makes Ordinary Control Freaks Look Like Stoned Hippies,' Says Former Engineer," *Business Insider*, October 12, 2011

[4] 1997 Letter to Shareholders, Jeff Bezos, Amazon.com, March 30, 1998.

Chapter 3

[1] "Fascinating Number: Amazon Is Larger Than The Next Dozen Internet Retailers Combined," *Forbes*, September 1, 2013.

[2] 2011 Letter to Shareholders, Jeff Bezos, Amazon.com, April 13, 2012.

[3] "Senior Software Development Manager, Item Authority," http://www.amazon.com/gp/jobs/221091, Amazon.com website

[4] "What is Fulfillment by Amazon (FBA)?" YouTube, July 17, 2013, (http://www.youtube.com/watch?v=IAi4fPb_kp4).

[5] 2011 Letter to Shareholders, Jeff Bezos, Amazon.com, April 13, 2012.

[6] "Private Cloud Matures, Hybrid Cloud is Next," Gartner, Inc., September 6, 2013.

[7] "Analyst: Amazon's Cloud Is Really A $19 Billion Business ... And Growing," *Business Insider*, January 7, 2013.

Chapter 4

[1] Charlie Rose, "Amazon's Jeff Bezos Looks to the Future," *60 Minutes*, December 1, 2013.

[2] "Inside Amazon's Idea Machine," *Forbes*, April 23, 2012.

[3] "Jeff Bezos, The Post's incoming owner, known for a demanding management style at Amazon," *The Washington Post*, August 7, 2013.

[4] George Anders, "Inside Amazon's Idea Machine," *Forbes*, April 23, 2012.

[5] http://www.amazon.com/gp/help/customer/display.html?modeId=12880481.

[6] "Seller Performance Management," http://www.amazon.com/gp/help/customer/display.html?nodeId=12880481, Amazon.com website

Chapter 5

[1] "Amazon.com Acquires Shoe E-tailer Zappos," *Bloomberg Businessweek*, July 22, 2009.

[2] Richard L. Brandt, One Click: Jeff Bezos and the Rise of Amazon.com, *Portfolio Trade*, December 31, 2012.

Chapter 6

[1] George Anders, "Inside Amazon's Idea Machine," *Forbes*, April 23, 2012.

[2] Marcus Wohlsen, "Amazon Outage Could Cost a Lot More Than 400,000 Pairs of Unsold Underwear," *Wired.com*, February 1, 2013.

[3] Brad Stone, *The Everything Store: Jeff Bezos and the Age of Amazon*, Little, Brown and Company, October 15, 2013.

Chapter 7

[1] "The Truth About Jeff Bezos' Amazing 10,000-Year Clock," *Business Insider*, August 12, 2013.

[2] "Jeff Bezos Interview," Academy of Achievement, May 4, 2001.

[3] 2012 Letter to Shareholders, Jeff Bezos, Amazon.com, April 12, 2012.

[4] Henry Blodget, "Amazon's Letter To Shareholders Should Inspire Every Company In America," *Business Insider*, April 14, 2013.

[5] Morgan Housel, "The 20 Smartest Things Jeff Bezos Has Ever Said," The Motley Fool, September 9, 2013.

[6] HBR IdeaCast, "Jeff Bezos on Leading for the Long-Term at Amazon," HBR Blog Network, January 3, 2013.

[7] 2004 Letter to Shareholders, Jeff Bezos, Amazon.com, April 13, 2004.

[8] 2012 Letter to Shareholders, Jeff Bezos, Amazon.com, April 12, 2012.

[9] "Jeff Bezos Interview," Academy of Achievement, May 4, 2001.

Chapter 8

[1] Alan Murray, *The Wall Street Journal Essential Guide to Management*, HarperBusiness, August 10, 2010.

[2] Morgan Housel, "The 20 Smartest Things Jeff Bezos Has Ever Said," The Motley Fool, September 9, 2013.

[3] Ibid.

Chapter 9

[1] "Bezos on Innovation," *BloombergBusinessweek*, April 18, 2008.

[2] "Jeff Bezos's Salary Is Only $14,000 More Than The Average Facebook Intern's," *Business Insider*, April 15, 2013.

[3] Brad Stone, *The Everything Store: Jeff Bezos and the Age of Amazon*, Little, Brown and Company, October 15, 2013.

[4] Ibid.

[5] Jim Edwards, "This Man Had Such A Bad Experience With Amazon Customer Support He Posted The Entire Conversation Online," *Business Insider*, December 3, 2013.

Chapter 10

[1] http://fulfillment.amazon.rtio.nl/amazon-fulfillment/leaders-of-fulfillment/miriam-park/

[2] Jim Collins, *How The Mighty Fall*, HarperBusiness, May 19, 2009.

[3] Jim Collins, *Good to Great*, HarperBusiness, October 16, 2001.

Chapter 11

[1] "How to Build (or Rebuild) Trust," www.michaelhyatt.com, April 16, 2012.

[2] 2011 Letter to Shareholders, Jeff Bezos, Amazon.com, April 13, 2012.

Chapter 12

[1] Fred Vogelstein, "Mighty Amazon," *Fortune*, May 26, 2003.

[2] http://www.charlierose.com/view/interview/12656.

[3] http://www.armedforcesjournal.com/essay-dumb-dumb-bullets/.

Chapter 13

[1] George Anders, "Bezos As a Media Tycoon: This is His Undeniable Agenda," Forbes, August 5, 2013.

[2] Amy Morin, "13 Things Mentally Strong People Don't Do," Lifehack.org, November 13, 2013.

[3] AL Duckworth, C Peterson, MD Matthews, DR Kelly, "Grit: Perseverance and Passion for Long-Term Goals," *Journal of Personality and Social Psychology*, 92 (6), 1087.

Conclusion

[1] "America's Best Leaders: Jeff Bezos, Amazom.com CEO," by David LaGesse, *US News & World Report*, November 19, 2008, http://www.usnews.com/news/best-leaders/articles/2008/11/19/americas-best-leaders-jeff-bezos-amazoncom-ceo.

Appendix A: Future Ready Self-Service

[1] "The Tide Has Turned: Nuance Research Finds Most Consumers Would Rather Self-Serve Over Speaking With a Live Agent," May 10, 2012, Nuance Communications, Inc.

[2] "3 Reasons to Show Your Support Page a Little Love," cccbuzz.exbdblogs.com, March 13, 2012.

[3] "Selecting Online Customer Service Channels To Satisfy Customers And Reduce Costs," Forrester Research Inc., June 25, 2010.

[4] 2011 Letter to Shareholders, Jeff Bezos, Amazon.com, April 13, 2012.

[5] "Stop Trying to Delight Your Customers," Matthew Dixon, Karen Freeman and Nicholas Toman, *Harvard Business Review*, July 2010.

[6] "Auto-Insurers Online Self-Service Report 2012: Leaders and Laggards," The Customer Respect Group, June 11, 2012.

[7] "Web Sites That Don't Support Customers Waste Millions," Forrester Research Inc., February 17, 2010.

[8] "The Business Impact of Customer Experience," Forrester Research, Inc., March 26, 2012.

[9] "An Unlikely Banker Emerges: Amazon," *The Wall Street Journal*, October 4, 2012.

Appendix B: Free Cash Flow

[1] http://www.usatoday.com/story/money/business/2013/10/31/what-jeff-bezos-gets-that-amazons-critics-dont/3324845/.

Appendix C: The Critical Capabilities of Building and Operating a Platform Company

[1] https://plus.google.com/+RipRowan/posts/eVeouesvaVX.
[2] http://pando.com/2013/07/23/move-fast-break-things-the-sad-story-of-platform-facebooks-gigantic-missed-opportunity/.